NIALL HORAN

NIALL HORAN

the unauthorized biography

DANNY WHITE

MICHAEL O'MARA BOOKS

First published in Great Britain in 2013 by
Michael O'Mara Books Limited
9 Lion Yard
Tremadoc Road
London SW4 7NQ

A CIP catalogue record for this book is available from the British Library.

Papers used by Michael O'Mara Books Limited are natural, recyclable
products made from wood grown in sustainable forests. The
manufacturing processes conform to the environmental regulations of
the country of origin.

ISBN 978-1-78243-185-5 in hardback print format
ISBN 978-1-78243-187-9 in trade paperback format
ISBN 978-1-78243-186-2 in ebook format

1 2 3 4 5 6 7 8 9 10

Jacket design by Ana Bježančević

Designed and typeset by Jack Clucas

Printed and bound by CPI Group (UK) Ltd, Croydon, CR0 4YY

www.mombooks.com

CONTENTS

INTRODUCTION

When athletes race around a running track, the spectators are often too busy focusing on the front-runners to notice that, on a few magical occasions, one of the less-fancied competitors has decided that he, too, has the right to be noticed. No longer will he merely make up the numbers. Putting his foot down, he finds to his delight that he can move to the front of the pack more easily than he could ever have imagined possible. The audience rises to its feet and roars in delight as a new star is born: who, after all, can resist the story of the outsider who finished first?

Niall Horan's is one such story – a tale that has warmed the heart of millions, including the king of pop, Justin Bieber. 'Good guys always win, bro' was the message that Justin sent to Niall after One Direction – or 1D, as they're sometimes called – had their first success in the American pop charts. For Niall, it was a defining message for two reasons: not only is the young Irishman a huge, longstanding fan of the Canadian singer, he also *is* a good guy. While One Direction's public-relations team is devoted to crafting a nice-guy image for each member of the band, with Niall this is the simplest of tasks – they just have to let him be his natural, charming self.

Visually, Niall's charms are no secret. His intense blue eyes offset a cherubic face, with his fair hair only adding to his angelic appeal. Yet this inherent innocence is diluted the moment his cheeky smile breaks out. That smile has changed during the course of his fame, as his much-discussed dental brace transformed his grin. Indeed, the toothy transformation has almost been a symbolic sign of his changing life. The angelic face of this alluring Irish boy – who grew up under the watchful eye of religious schools – is no mask. At heart, 'Nialler' is a wholesome, if cheeky, young man.

Watching Niall adjust to the almost claustrophobic level of fame of his band – and the colourful temptations that come with it – has been particularly fascinating. He has felt, at times, cramped both physically and metaphorically by the pressure of it all. His natural demeanour – laid-back, kind and sometimes clownish – has been strongly tested by the intensity of One Direction's popularity. Yet with the pressure and intensity have come so much fun, fame and fortune.

The music of One Direction has topped the charts in countries Niall didn't even know existed before he joined the band. His life nowadays is a merry hop between sold-out venues full of adoring fans, luxury hotels, show-business gatherings and recording studios. His personal wealth is estimated to be in the region of at least £5 million. His every dream has been exceeded. He admits that, as a child, he sang in the shower but he never believed that he would end up with a record deal, let alone in an all-conquering pop sensation. Sometimes he has to pinch himself.

Niall's journey within the One Direction story is certainly the most intriguing. He was initially considered a 'bookend' member of the band by some and, crueller still, was mocked over elements of his appearance, including his teeth. While other members, most notably the much-discussed Harry Styles, attracted more attention than Niall, the young Irish lad continued to believe in himself and to play his part in the band. Then, like something from a fairytale, he suddenly found his popularity within the group increasing. His newfound stature first showed its head in the United States, yet soon the rest of the world's

'Directioners' were awakening to the charm of Niall. Some had always loved him most, of course. For them, watching the sudden stampede in the direction of Niall was a bittersweet experience.

For Niall, too, there have been highs and lows, victories and setbacks, in both his career and life beyond it. The only thing that has been lacking in Niall's life since he became famous has been the chance to relax and take some time out. Throughout it all, those little things that make Niall so charming have remained true, as he has elegantly made the transition from an unknown Irish boy to a world-famous superstar. He is pop's Mr Nice Guy, and here is his story. And, to paraphrase the title of one of his band's songs, it is the best story ever.

CHAPTER ONE

IN THE BEGINNING . . .

Niall James Horan was born on 13 September 1993. He was raised by his mother Maura and father Bobby in the town of Mullingar, in the county of Westmeath, Ireland. He has a brother called Greg, who is six years older. For the first four years of Niall's life, the Horan family lived on a street in the centre of the town and his earliest memories include fun days spent playing with his toy tractor on the street. During these formative years, Niall spent most of his time trailing along with his brother and his friends, as the area they lived in was short of kids Niall's age, which meant he learned that he needed to work hard to be noticed and accepted. Greg, when asked by the *Herald* newspaper to describe the family in which Niall grew up, said, 'We were just ordinary people.' This is a simple definition but a fine one: Niall was every inch both the small-town boy and the classic younger sibling, wandering wide-eyed in the wake of his big brother.

Some people believe that the order in which a person is born into their family – as first, middle, last or only child – has a significant effect on their character and their experience of life. Niall is in the group known as 'last-borns' – the children who tend to enjoy being the centre of attention. As the American author and expert on developmental psychology Linda Blair puts it in her influential book *Birth Order*, 'Last borns have an outgoing, charming and cute nature – they're often the entertainers when they're with other people.' As anyone who has seen One Direction interviewed will know, Blair's words describe Niall accurately. They were true of his behaviour as a child, too. She also argues that last-borns are often both creative and willing to take risks. On a less positive note, they are vulnerable to feelings of inferiority and low self-esteem and can feel disappointed easily. They can also be manipulative. We will occasionally revisit each of these tendencies as Niall's story unfolds in the chapters ahead.

For several years, Niall and Greg 'hated' each other and, says Niall, found each other 'annoying'. This was, as

Niall tells it, a little more than just everyday sibling tension common to many families. 'I hated it whenever he looked at me,' wrote Niall in the official One Direction book, *Dare To Dream: Life as One Direction*, 'and we used to fight all the time.' This was a less than ideal situation for Niall as the younger and smaller of the two. However, the younger brother proved he could be the plucky underdog when, on one occasion during a particularly boisterous scrap, Niall struck Greg with a table-tennis bat, drawing blood. A happier memory is of the Christmas when Niall was given a Scalextric car track. He was so excited as he pulled the wrapping paper off the large box and discovered the toy inside. 'I must have been about four or five years old and I got a Scalextric thing and that was probably one of the best presents I ever got,' he told Capital FM. The family had two pet goldfish they named after the cartoon characters Tom and Jerry. Tragically, both fish died after Greg accidentally overfed them. It was a grievous day for the Horan brothers.

Mullingar, the town in which Niall was born and grew up, was founded by the Normans over 800 years ago. It has enjoyed a roller-coaster existence of highs and lows, yet during the final two decades of the twentieth century, during which Niall was born, Mullingar's population almost trebled and improved transport links made it almost a suburb of greater Dublin. The town is very proud of its famous pop son and boasts a fine tradition of being the birthplace of many singers, writers and artists. The singer Joe Dolan and musician Niall Breslin both came from the town, as do former pop stars the Swarbriggs and the soprano Ailish Tynan. The renowned author James Joyce had connections with the town and mentioned it in one of his most famous novels, *Ulysses*; and the poet and once-time Poet Laureate Sir John Betjeman also visited. Now, the town's ambassadors and tourist officers proudly push the Horan connection to the hilt. Some particularly dedicated Directioners have taken holidays there purely on the strength of their hero's origins.

As a kid, Niall enjoyed dressing up for fun as a kid. A photograph shows him at the age of four dressed in a camouflage army outfit, holding a rifle. His sweet face and cute smile form a striking contrast to the military gear. Another photo shows him with a toy guitar and microphone, performing in the family living room. In another shot, he was snapped dressed up in a red Teletubbies outfit.

Around the time of his fourth birthday, young Niall got a taste of the life that was ahead of him as a pop star when the family flew to America to visit his aunt. One can only imagine Niall's excitement as he stepped onto the plane that would whisk his family to New York. How big and brash everything in Manhattan must have seemed to the diminutive four-year-old! Could the iconic skyscrapers and atmosphere of energetic ambition that the city runs on have inspired the young Irish boy even then to make something special of his life? He has given no hints. 'I was there when I was a kid,' Niall recalled on Twitter. 'My aunt lives in Queens, Woodside.' (He was not the only member of One Direction to visit the States as a child: Liam Payne flew there on several occasions during his childhood and adolescence.)

It was an exciting trip for Niall, yet he soon came crashing down when, within months of the family's return to Ireland, his parents' marriage finally broke under the strain of a prolonged period of disharmony. It took some years for Niall and his brother to settle with one parent. 'They divorced when I was about five. I was young at the time, so I kind of moved between houses,' he later told the *Sunday World*. As is often the case, the brothers first went to live with their mother, Maura, but for the next few years they moved between her home and their father Bobby's place. Eventually, they chose to settle with Bobby, who was very relieved to have them with him. 'They came home one night and that was it: they told me they'd decided to stay,' he later told the *Daily Mirror*. 'I was very lonely for that year without them, so of course I was really happy to have them back. I had a family around me again.'

Astrologically, Niall is a Virgo. People born under this sign are, according to astrology's adherents, industrious, methodical and efficient. They can also be analytical, observant, helpful, reliable and precise. The more delicate of these traits are the ones that are most commonly attributed to Niall. 'He has a very soft side to him,' said his father. 'His mother taught him to bake . . . he can do cupcakes. He had to look after himself a lot because I was working, so from the age of seven he had to do his own washing, his own ironing and often his own cooking.' Bobby believes that all children at that age should be so qualified. 'When he was at school I tried to get home for 4.30 p.m., but I started early mornings, so Niall had to get himself up and walk the mile and a half to school,' said his dad.

Although Niall's new home was an all-male affair, there was always a healthy slice of maternal influence in his life. 'They lived with me but their mother was very involved and we made decisions together,' Bobby told the *Daily Mirror*. 'Niall always had two birthday parties . . . one here and one at his mum's and whenever she wanted to see them she would come over.' The siblings' decision to live with their father had a great deal to do with the location of Bobby's home. It was more central and therefore more convenient for Niall to get to his primary school. He attended the St Kenny National School. Formed in 1980 as an amalgamation of three smaller establishments, St Kenny is a Roman Catholic School which, according to its own literature, 'aims at promoting the full and harmonious development of all aspects of the person of the pupil, intellectual, physical, cultural, moral and spiritual, including a living relationship with God and with other people'. To be clear, then, this is a firmly religious establishment that 'models and promotes a philosophy of life inspired by belief in God and in the life, death and resurrection of Jesus Christ'. It is named after a Gaelic abbot from the early medieval period who was also a monastic founder, priest and missionary.

Like a lot of children, young Niall eventually grew to love school, but he absolutely loathed his first day there. When Maura dropped him off he burst into tears. He did not want to be parted from his mother and did not want to spend the day at this unfamiliar and initially scary place. To make the experience even harder, none of Niall's friends were joining the same school as he was. To Niall, the prospect of years ahead of him in this strange place seemed less than appealing. 'I was so scared of being all on my own,' he wrote in *Dare To Dream*. He was sometimes a lonely child away from school, as well. This was partly due to the aforementioned considerable gap in years between him and Greg, and partly as a result of his parents' divorce. He dealt with this in various ways, including the creation of an imaginary friend. 'I used to have an imaginary friend named Michael,' he has admitted in *Dare to Dream*. He also developed a people-pleasing streak, a move that he believes was partly prompted by his small height. He also explains how he avoided being bullied for his lack of height. 'I tried to be friendly to everyone,' he wrote. 'I was always up for having a laugh and messing around, so I got on really well with most of the other kids.' It was in these years that Niall's ability and tendency to charm were honed. Put simply, he learned to deal with fears of ostracism by turning on the charm. This skill would serve him well when he became famous.

Once he had settled at school, Niall grew to enjoy almost all aspects of it. But he remained a remorseless chatterbox, talking 'a lot during lessons', he later admitted in the official One Direction autobiography. His favourite subjects were French and Geography, but he was less keen on English and Maths. Apart from homework, which, like many kids, he was not a fan of, Niall loved most of the educational experience. His naughtier moments included the time he bunked a day off school and got into trouble when he was caught. On another occasion, during a particularly boring geography class another boy broke wind loudly. He and Niall both fell about laughing and, as a result of this untimely emission, became firm friends. (Niall has been credited by his bandmates as the most flatulent member of One Direction.) The two were instant soulmates. They would sit at the back of the class fooling around and singing traditional Irish folk songs. Sometimes a third boy, also called Niall, would join them in their back-row banter. Wit was much valued in these sessions, with the three boys vying to make each other laugh. Amusing, amused and flatulent, Niall finally felt as if he belonged somewhere.

But the terrible trio's cheeky rapport caused endless frustration for teachers who would, Niall remembered, be 'raging at us'. In general, the staff felt that Niall was not fulfilling his potential. He got, he says, 'OK' grades and was told by teachers had he had a great deal of potential. However, by his own admission he was 'too busy messing around or playing football with my mates to really get down to work'. Indeed, at one parents' evening, a teacher told Maura that Niall was always in a world of his own during lessons. On one occasion, described in *Dare to Dream*, Niall was suspended from secondary school. He has been rather vague about the details, but finally disclosed some of them during an interview with a US radio station. 'I maybe stole something when I was at school, like stuff off a friend,' he said. 'I was not a bad boy but I got suspended for two days for general messing about. I talked too much, which probably got me in trouble.'

Niall became increasingly fond of the creative side of the school curriculum. Within months of starting primary school, he began to learn to play the recorder. 'I got really into it,' he wrote. He also loved the singing classes. Each Christmas the school would have a carol concert, and Niall stood out every time. With his cherubic face and sweet voice, he certainly looked and sounded the part of the classical choirboy. It was a teacher called Anne Caulfield who first noted Niall's vocal ability. However, she says it was his personality that charmed her as much as his voice. 'He is remembered for his manners and his personality as much as his singing,' she told the *Irish Independent*. The bantering, grunting boy of geography classes transformed into a more angelic creature in music lessons. 'He was a little saintly child in the classroom and every other teacher would say the same. A very, very good boy.' She suggested to the very, very good boy that he audition for the town's choir. Indeed, Niall's family remember that, during his primary-school years, he began to sing more and more. His confidence was growing all the time, as he became quite different from the trembling, upset boy who had been dropped off for his first day of schooling. He was finding that his increasingly affable, charismatic personality, combined with his sweet singing voice, was enough to win people over. This discovery would help transport him to his destiny as a world-famous pop singer.

His America-based aunt can remember the moment that she first believed he would meet that destiny. She would visit the family every summer and join them on holiday in Galway, in the west of Ireland. As they were driving along during one such holiday, Niall, sitting in the back of the car, began singing a Garth Brooks song. So strong was Niall's voice that his aunt did not even realize he was singing – she assumed the radio was switched on. When she became aware that it was her nephew's voice she could hear, she was impressed, and says now that it was that moment she realized what a future he had ahead of him. Curiously, a very similar experience happened when popular jazz singer Michael Bublé was a child. On that occasion, Bublé, whom Niall now variously describes as his 'man crush' and his 'absolute hero', was singing 'White Christmas' in the back of a car. It was then that the Canadian's father noticed his son's immense vocal talent.

Niall's aunt told him then, and many times in the years ahead, that he was going to become a famous singer. Although Niall mostly shrugged off her excited predictions, her confidence in him will have had an effect. When he discovered the Bublé coincidence he was more than tickled. It was around this time that the fates began to smile down on Niall. In Britain, ITV was launching *Pop Idol*, its search for a new pop star. The show's star judge was a previously unknown record executive called Simon Cowell, and he and Niall would get to know each other very well in the years to come.

When he was nine years old, Niall stepped out onto the stage for the first time when he performed as the lead in a school production of *Oliver!*. 'I just always remember being happy on stage,' Niall recalls. As he stepped out in his costume he looked quite the part of the hapless orphan. 'He had the lead part in *Oliver!* in 2004, he was in fourth class,' school principal Arthur Fallon recalls. 'I remember that song "Where is Love?". He sang that song. It's a very difficult song, and he sang it and it was very moving.' According to the *Irish Independent*, in *Forever Young* Niall recalled that his performance 'went down well', adding, 'I really began to enjoy being in front of an audience.' Whenever he had the chance to perform a bit of karaoke, Niall grabbed the opportunity and sang the Frank Sinatra track 'Fly Me to the Moon'. (Coincidentally, his future bandmate Liam Payne had sung the same song at his first *X Factor* audition in 2008, two years before the series in which One Direction was formed. That was when he made it to the judges'-house phase in the fifth series, but Cowell thought Liam wasn't quite ready and suggested he come back in two years' time. He did!)

*

By the time Niall moved to secondary school, he was already becoming more and more creative. He attended the Catholic secondary school Coláiste Mhuire in Mullingar, primarily a boys' school, but with some levels that are coeducational. Unlike his primary school, which was a relatively new establishment, Coláiste Mhuire first opened its doors in 1856. 'We strive to create a positive, orderly and caring environment which will nurture the talents and potential of all in our school community,' boasts its official website. A less explicitly religious mission statement than the one promoted by Niall's primary school, yet his secondary school continued the faith-based atmosphere of his childhood. Many of the values and qualities that are so strong in Niall, and that have seen him respond with such grace to the monstrous fame he has acquired, were instilled in him here.

At the age of twelve, in perhaps the most significant development of his secondary-school years, Niall learned to play the guitar. He referred to his first instrument as 'the best present I ever received for Christmas' – even more exciting than his Scalextric. He decided to go down the self-taught route, learning his chords, strumming and picking patterns from the Internet. He was on his way to musical superstardom.

Just one year later, he entered a local talent show, in a foreshadow of the televisual audition that would later change his life. He sang the song 'The Man Who Can't Be Moved' by the Script. The mellow Irish tones of the band's vocalist, Danny O'Donoghue, were ones that Niall could replicate well. His friend Kieron accompanied Niall on guitar at the audition. Although the show he appeared at was not a competition in the strictest sense, being a part of it had boosted Niall's confidence. The local media had sent reporters and photographers to the event and Niall was thrilled to see photographs of himself in the local newspapers. It was such a buzz to have that fame, and he proudly showed the reports to his family and friends.

He then entered a small talent show that did have a competitive dimension. Again, he rolled up with a guitar-clutching Kieron at his side, but this time he sang Chris Brown's 'With You'. In moving from indie rock to R&B, Niall was showing a sense of versatility even at this early stage. The audience reportedly lapped up the performance and rewarded it with hearty applause. Some even asked Niall for his autograph, sensing perceptively that they had a future star in front of them.

To their delight, Niall and Kieron won the show. Niall has recalled that he found it 'amazing' to finish on top and how this made him believe that, perhaps, singing could be something he could make a career of. That said, the family were disappointed when the local newspaper failed to print the photograph they had taken of Niall and Kieron with the trophy. Niall's grandmother even phoned the newspaper to complain about the omission. A far cry from nowadays, when he is not short of column inches.

Two months later, Niall entered yet another show, the Mullingar Shamrocks' 'Stars in Their Eyes' contest, singing the Jason Mraz hit 'I'm Yours'. His interest in becoming a professional singer was growing. The reception his performances were getting only served to boost his ambition and self-belief, although he was also considering other arms of the entertainment industry. 'Niall was always interested in showbiz,' Bobby told the *Irish Independent*. 'Apart from singing, he's always spent his childhood mimicking others. He's brilliant . . . he can pick up any dialect.' Elsewhere, he has stated that Niall's ability to impersonate accents is so strong 'he could probably do a better Geordie accent than Cheryl Cole', adding that his son is 'very witty and good-humoured'.

However, while he was working well on his singing talent, Niall's progress on his visual style was less successful. He got a 'V' shape shaved into the back of his neck one day but left the hair on the side longer, to create a peculiar look. It seemed a good idea at the time but he has since concluded in *Dare to Dream* that it looked 'disgusting on me'. He knows now that such errors are all part of growing up but feels that his hair and sometimes wardrobe malfunctions were 'particularly bad'. However, Bobby remembers his son's sartorial efforts more fondly. 'He always dressed himself well and had a nice style about him. He never left the house without making sure he looked good,' said the proud father in the *Daily Mirror*.

Perhaps his 'interesting' looks during his early teens contributed to his lack of romantic relationships, although Niall has suggested this might have been more of a conscious decision on his part. While he says he had his first kiss as the age of eleven, he adds that it was a disappointing and underwhelming experience. 'I think I've blocked it out of my mind because it was so bad,' he writes. 'I'm not sure it even counts as a kiss.' He explained separately that the lucky recipient was a foreign-exchange student visiting from France. 'She was actually staying at my friend's house,' he told the Sugarscape website. 'I got to know her and I ended up kissing her.' He then dated a girl for a short while after he turned thirteen. When compared with the reportedly ever-eventful love life of his bandmate Harry Styles, Niall's romantic backstory is tame. 'I've not actually been on too many dates,' he has told *OK!* magazine. 'I just like sitting at home, chilling and watching a movie,' he added. That said, few young men can rival the reputed conquests of Styles.

Much of the official One Direction narrative offers a sanitized view of Niall's childhood. A less polished glimmer into his hopes for the future can be found on his old page on the social-networking website Bebo, on which he wrote that he wanted kids and hoped to get married one day. His career dream was to 'work in some way in America'. Under his list of fears, he wrote that he was scared of dying, being scraped by a 'certain someone's nails' and being 'kicked in the balls by the same person'. He also wrote:

> Me, Myself, and I … ari everybod! ….. the name is niall. im 16 .. im in 5th year in mary's … singin is my life do nothin else! ….. im always up for a laff ….. so if u know me or wanna know me leave uz a comment and do my blogs girls ….. .. cya later bud.

As part of perhaps the first-ever generation whose childhoods are entirely documented on online social networking websites, Niall has quite a 'virtual trail'. None of it is scandalous, though, nor is any of it embarrassing in any painful sense of the word.

During his childhood, Niall developed a fear of birds, particularly pigeons, which he has been fairly open about. 'I can't stand them after one once flew in through my bathroom window and went for me while I was having a wee, he told the *Sun*. 'That was enough. I think pigeons target me.' Fear of birds, known as ornithophobia, is common, with pigeons featuring prominently. When confronted by birds, some phobics suffer from extreme symptoms such as heart palpitations, sweating and anxiety. For others, the fear shows itself most strongly in avoidance of situations in which they might come across birds, and Niall's bandmates do their best to take care of him when pigeons are nearby. For the phobic to focus on a particular bird is not uncommon: while Niall focuses on pigeons, the rapper Eminem is scared of owls.

Farts, bird fear, laughter, impersonations and dodgy haircuts – Niall's was an entertaining and, at times, amusing adolescence. As he bounced back from the heartache of watching his parents divorce, Niall began to really love life again. Most of all, he loved making music. Summing up his childhood, he said later, 'I was always the kid that picked up the nearest instrument and just loved music.' Rich in satisfaction is the young man who can carve out a career doing what he loves. Niall would in time become rich in many ways.

CHAPTER TWO

HE'S GOT THE X FACTOR

Niall's journey to the very top of the music industry might seem to some outsiders to have been remarkably effortless. However, in reality, it has involved lots of work and several twists and turns along the way. As Niall became more serious (and noisy) about his guitar playing, Bobby decided that things had to change. He was concerned that Niall's relentless practising would soon drive the neighbours wild. Indeed, on Niall's own Bebo profile he had written that he loved 'buzz blarin the tunes (then the neighbours go mad)'. Dutifully, his father converted the garage at the bottom of the garden into a new bedroom for his youngest son, and Niall was hardly put out by the move, as it had provided him with the biggest room in the household. It almost felt as if he now had his own home and, accordingly, he set about personalizing the place. Two of the walls were painted red, the other two blue, and Niall adorned them with signed football posters – one from Newcastle United's Danny Simpson, another from Derby County's Jamie Ward. As a football fanatic, Niall loved these items and gave them pride of place.

'I love football so much,' Niall would later tweet. 'I will watch anything!' He is a Derby County fan, like his father Bobby, and he attended his first match at just four years of age. On one exciting day, Bobby and Niall travelled to England, as Niall had been chosen to be a mascot for a Derby County match at Luton Town. It was a thrilling experience for the twelve-year-old. His listing in the match-day programme explained that Niall's favourite player was Tommy Smith, who was voted the club's player of the year in 2006. As Bobby would later tell the *Sun*, 'He loved being their mascot. Walking out in front of crowds was good training for what he's doing today.' In a photograph of Niall and the other mascots lined up alongside the two teams' captains the little Irish boy looks beyond excited.

Niall's football fanaticism also dictated his choice of

username for his account on Bebo, for which he chose 'init_ to_win_it_dcfc' – the last four letters representing Derby County Football Club – as his moniker (his username for MSN was, embarrassingly enough, da_pimp_is_here_@ hotmail.com). Niall enjoyed *playing* football, too, though one day he picked up an injury, which haunts him to this day. 'I dislocated my knee playing football one time and when I got checked by the specialist I was told I've got a 67 per cent chance of walking down the street and my knee dislocating itself,' he told the *Daily Mirror*. One report suggested he has, since the injury first struck, dislocated it on at least thirteen occasions.

Meanwhile, Niall's almost obsessive love of music was growing all the time. At the age of ten, he attended his first concert when he went to see the three-piece UK band Busted, at a time when the influential pop-punk-lite band, featuring Charlie Simpson, James Bourne and Matt Willis, were at the very peak of their powers. Standing among a screaming audience as the boy band performed on stage will have swelled Niall's imagination of how it felt to be actually on stage, provoking, rather than emitting, the screams. Even if he did dream of being in their place, he could have little comprehended how he would soon eclipse the popularity of even Busted in their prime.

At this time, Niall was also adding to his CD collection,

with the greatest-hits album of the American rockers Bon Jovi an early favourite. On his Bebo profile he listed his favourite acts as Michael Bublé, the Eagles, Frank Sinatra, the Script and the Coronas – a mixed bag of bands and artists that showed how wide his tastes were even back then. Together, these bands were fuelling Niall's imagination and creativity. Swing acts especially, including both modern-day artists such as Bublé and more classic crooners like Sinatra, were a major influence on the impressionable teen. 'Bublé is a big inspiration for me because he has a great voice, can write a song, has a great ear for music, and demands your attention when he's performing,' he later told media site IrishCentral. 'When I was growing up, I was a big swing [music] fan, so I'm big into Frank Sinatra and Dean Martin,' he added. His favourite album of all time is *Crazy Love* by Bublé.

Gradually, fate was moving Niall closer to his destiny. In 2009, he had his first brush with the television show that would propel him to fame the following year, when he was handed the opportunity to open for the former *X Factor* finalist Lloyd Daniels at a small Dublin venue called Academy 2. Young Welshman Daniels had entered the show in 2009, and, although he reached the live shows, he had not been snapped up by a major record label. Niall was excited to get the chance to perform to Daniels's fanbase, having enjoyed watching the Welshman's progress on the series. Sitting on a stool, wearing a baseball cap back to front, with his acoustic guitar on his lap, Niall sang hits including Justin Bieber's 'Baby', his favourite song as a schoolboy. His performance was good, although he ran through it a little quickly and lacked the polish that was evident in his technique the following year. He also sang Justin Timberlake's 'Cry Me a River', and the crowd in the venue, which has a capacity of 850 people, reacted favourably.

Backstage, Niall chatted with Daniels and asked him all about his experiences on *The X Factor*. Part of their conversation has since become a matter of dispute. Niall recalls that, when he told Daniels of his own ambition to audition on the show in the future, the Welshman was dismissive and unimpressed by the idea. Later, when Niall and One Direction were romping through the live shows of *The X Factor*, Daniels visited the studio. On seeing Niall, he said, 'See, I told you to go for it!' But Niall insists in *Dare to Dream* that Daniels had, in fact, done no such thing.

However, Daniels's experience with the show is actually an interesting case study for what could have befallen Niall when he later auditioned. The young Welshman seemed to have plenty going for him to appeal to the large teenage sector of *The X Factor* audience: he was young and he had cute, boyish good looks, of just the kind that appeal to teenagers. His voice was good and he carried at least a certain amount of charisma and personality. In his first audition, Cheryl Cole told him he was 'the first person I'm going to say you've got the X factor to'. So far, so good. But, while all of this was enough to carry him through the boot-camp and judges'-houses stages of the competition, once he reached the live shows he began to falter. He was in the bottom two for two weeks before finally exiting the competition in fifth place.

Since leaving the show, he has struggled to make any impact on the music industry. He retains a reasonable fanbase, boasting 187,531 followers on Twitter as of June 2013, and has performed live at some small events. However, even for such modest success, Daniels has had to work extremely hard. His case showed that even good-looking boys are not guaranteed success as a result of *The X Factor*. Daniels would, in retrospect, have stood a much greater chance of making a proper impact had he been part of a band. Indeed, his look would have fitted into One Direction well. By sticking rigidly to the solo option, Daniels showed Niall and the other future members of One Direction how tough the industry can be, even for those who have, on the face of it, plenty going for them. Could

Niall have faced a similar fate had *The X Factor* bosses not given him the chance to join a band? We will never know, but it is plausible that he might have.

Meanwhile, as he prepared for his own *X Factor* audition, sixteen-year-old Niall had been dating a girl in Ireland. As ever, he has been coy about the details, stating only on entertainment website Sugarscape that she was 'amazing'. Thankfully, his mum, Maura, filled in a few gaps during an interview with the *Herald* newspaper. 'He had a girlfriend at home, from his school days, before he auditioned for *X Factor*,' she said. 'But then he was doing that and she was doing exams, so life is very different for him now. I don't know if he sees much of her when he's home, she was lovely, but they were only sixteen at the time – there's never anything too steady about a relationship at that age.' Bobby, too, has suggested that Niall does not have a crowded romantic curriculum vitae. 'He never really brought girls home,' Bobby told *Heat* magazine. 'He had some girls that were friends and they would all sit on the wall outside together, but that was all. 'He's never had a real girlfriend ... he went to an all-boys' school so it was hard to meet girls.'

One wonders how much embarrassment Niall must have felt to see his parents discussing his private life with high-circulation publications. Most teenage boys would cringe in such circumstances. There seems to be no territory that his parents will not step into, as Bobby showed when he even discussed whether or not he believes his son is a virgin. 'I don't believe he's a virgin,' he said in May 2012. 'I couldn't say, and I wasn't in the house all the time, so I don't really know what went on when I wasn't there.' How strange Niall must have felt when he realized that millions of fans were poring over his father's speculation over such a tender matter!

The girl Niall had dated was called Holly Scally. She has since opened up about the circumstances that led to their breaking up. 'We were apart for four weeks, which felt really long because we used to see each other all the time,' she told *NOW* magazine. 'One day, Niall called and said, "I think we should finish because I never see you." I said, "Yeah, I know. I understand." So it's cool.'I think he felt bad because he kept saying, "I'm so sorry." I tried to sound like it was no big deal but it was a bit sad for me.'

They stayed in touch to a degree and would sometimes chat online via Skype. It is no wonder she was upset by the split, for she describes romantic behaviour from Niall during their time together. 'He was lovely – funny, cheeky and kind,' she said. 'He was also very affectionate – we always called each other "babe" and he'd always end his texts with a kiss. It was all very innocent but he was very good kisser!' It is enough to make any Directioner jealous.

It gets yet more romantic. When they were short of money, which was often, Niall still did his best to treat Holly well. 'On one date Niall took me to Roma Café in Mullingar for some chips, which probably only cost about two euros [£1.60],' she said. Fittingly, he would even serenade his girlfriend. 'Even back then I knew he'd go far, he was always singing and playing his guitar and he was really good,' said Scally. 'He used to sing me songs he'd written or covers, like Justin Bieber's "Baby" or Jason Mraz's "I'm Yours". Once he paid 15 euros [£12] to hire a boat and rowed me across a lake while singing to me.'

Although she and Niall split before One Direction were formed, like many young ladies connected to a member of the band she would face unpleasant times as the band's popularity rose.

Compared with all this open chatter, Niall has been guarded about his own taste in girls. He is generally private about his romantic affairs. However, he has offered hints as to what he prefers in a young woman. He has said he likes girls without makeup and has also suggested he likes shy girls. Niall also admires girls who can mimic different accents or speak different languages, and he has said he is generally after a girl who eats just as much as he does and that he finds a girl who can play guitar hard to resist.

True to his Catholic upbringing, he has said he does

not believe in sex before marriage. He is a touch partial to having his hair played with by girls. 'I like the older woman,' he has also said to IrishCentral. As we shall see, he is not the only member of One Direction with such a preference. He has also quipped that, such is his love of pizza, he would rather eat a slice of it than kiss a girl. Niall has added that he let his relationship with Holly go because he wanted to concentrate on the challenge ahead with *The X Factor*. 'I needed to concentrate on my career,' he said. This gives a hint of a side of him that is not immediately apparent amid his fondness for tomfoolery. Niall is, when he wants to be, a hugely focused individual. True also to his star sign of Virgo, he can methodically and determinedly focus on a challenge, part of which involves putting aside anything that could distract him from his goal.

Niall had begun to study for his leaving certificate, Ireland's final school exams. His initial plan was to go to university and study sound engineering. He had plans to move into the music industry in some capacity, and felt that being adept at the controls of recording studio and mixing desks would give him a head start. While he wanted to make it as a star in the industry, he was realistic enough to understand that he might have to settle for being more of a 'crew member' than a 'leading light'. Such pragmatism is refreshing among those who audition for reality shows.

Too often such aspiring stars proceed on the basis that their life depends on winning the show and getting a record deal; these expressions of desperation have begun to grate with many viewers. Niall's more grounded approach adds to his charm in the eyes of the public.

Niall was also taking a similarly sensible approach to his forthcoming *X Factor* bid. His lack of desperation, shared in the main by his future bandmates, would prove a significant boost to his appeal. The public has had its fill of crazy-eyed, desperate youngsters explaining over and over to *X Factor* cameras that 'this means more than anything to me'! What the public want is a more down-to-earth and charming approach, and in the shape of Niall they were about to get the perfect candidate. Summing up his son in the *Daily Mirror*, Bobby said, 'He's a real gent, a lovely, well-mannered, well-brought-up lad'.

The fame Niall was about to acquire would be huge. It would bring money and lots of excitement, but challenges, too. Because it all came so swiftly, staying true to his well-grounded and polite ways would be an almost ever-present challenge, since there would always seem to be a new temptation to compromise his principles.

Niall decided to apply for *The X Factor* after watching the climax of the sixth series of the show in December 2009.

The final two were baby-faced Geordie Joe McElderry and Essex likely lad Olly Murs. Niall was particularly interested in McElderry's fate because, at eighteen, the Geordie was the youngest ever finalist and, as such, the closest in age to Niall. The fact that a teenager had made it all the way to the final, and was eventually crowned winner, encouraged Niall. That evening he decided he would give *The X Factor* a shot himself. Perhaps, he hoped, he could follow in McElderry's footsteps and win. At the end of the show, the application process for the 2010 series was announced. Niall took down the details and applied. After filling in the form, he tweeted to his friends, 'Applied for xfactor, hope it all works out.' These words seem rather poignant given what has happened since.

It would be months before the audition process began, so Niall continued to practise in the hope that he could continue to improve in time for the big day. The initial auditions were held at Croke Park in 2010, a sports stadium in central Dublin. Like all potential contestants, Niall first had to sing in front of the production team, who would decide whether he would be invited back to sing in front of the cameras and the famous judging panel. No decision was given to him on the day – he was merely told the producers would be in touch in due course. The next few weeks were tense for Niall, as he awaited the phone call that he had begun to think would never come. Then, while he was on holiday in Spain, the call finally arrived – *The X Factor* wanted Niall to audition in front of the judges! He could hardly contain his excitement.

On the eve of the big day, Niall stayed overnight with his cousin in Dublin so he could get to the stadium easily the next morning, but he was so nervous and excited that he could not sleep. The following day, he arrived at the Dublin Convention Centre at 5 a.m., shaking with nerves. 'I was absolutely bricking it,' he later wrote in *Dare to Dream*. Taking in the thousands of other hopefuls lining up to audition, Niall concluded he had no hope of succeeding. Standing near him in the queue was a young man called Jordan O'Keefe. Although O'Keefe was unsuccessful on the day, three years later he would audition for *Britain's Got Talent* and blow the audience away with his performance of 'Little Things' by One Direction. Following his encounter with Niall, Jordan later told the *Sun*, 'We were stood next to each other and he was playing his guitar. I asked if I could borrow it to play something. We got chatting.'

Back in Dublin on the big day, Niall was chosen to be interviewed by the show's host Dermot O'Leary before his audition – an early sign that the producers anticipated big things for the young Irishman. Speaking to O'Leary, Niall mentioned that he had been compared to Justin Bieber and added, 'It's not a bad comparison.' He said he wanted to sell out arenas, record albums and work with 'some of the best artists in the world'. He said that his audition was the starting point of all that. 'If I get through today, it's game on!' he said, throwing down the gauntlet.

It was a striking introduction to the world – and he certainly did not want for charm or confidence. As he strolled onto the stage and stood in front of the judging panel that comprised Simon Cowell, Cheryl Cole, Louis Walsh and guest judge Katy Perry, he announced casually, 'All right, Dublin?' showing little sign of his nerves.

Louis Walsh asked his fellow Irishman what had brought him to the competition. 'I'm here today to be the best artist I can be in the world,' he replied. Niall's qualification that he wanted to be the best he could be, rather than just the best, showed how, even in his wildest dreams and ambitions, he retained a healthy slice of grounded self-awareness.

Walsh then asked Niall if he was the 'Irish Justin Bieber', to which the future star agreed. After his chat with Louis, Niall traded banter with Katy Perry, saying, half in jest, that he had entered the show to become more popular with girls. It showed some confidence that he could be so at ease with a world-famous, not to mention strikingly gorgeous, singer such as Perry.

With the pleasantries over, it was time for Niall to

perform. He began by singing the well-known Jason Mraz song 'I'm Yours'. But, unfortunately for Niall, Cowell had heard too many people audition with this track in recent years, and he interrupted Niall's performance to tell him it was a lazy song choice and asked if he had a second song to perform instead. Luckily, Niall did – 'So Sick' by Ne-Yo. Interestingly, Justin Bieber had performed this song at the *Stratford Star* talent contest in Ontario, which, indirectly, made him famous. But, while Bieber had sung it convincingly and with emotion, Niall seemed curiously detached during his performance of it. His eyes seemed glued to the back of the venue as he sang, in contrast to his future bandmates, who would mostly direct their attention to the judging panel during their respective auditions.

Again, Cowell interrupted Niall's audition before he had a chance to finish the song. Katy Perry was the first to offer feedback. 'I think you're adorable!' she told Niall. 'You've got charisma. I just think that maybe you should work on it. You're only sixteen; I started out when I was fifteen and I didn't make it until I was twenty-three.' The American, it seemed, was sitting on the fence. Cowell's response, too, was rather mixed. 'I think you're unprepared. I think you came with the wrong song, you're not as good as you thought you were, but I still like you,' he told Niall. When even the straight-talking, black-and-white king of reality television is hedging his bets, you know you've delivered an uncommon audition.

Cheryl Cole's verdict came next and, since she was Niall's favourite female celebrity, Cole's verdict was one he was keen to hear. The Geordie pop star, a graduate of the reality-television sphere herself, said, 'Yeah, you're obviously adorable. You've got a lot of charm for a sixteen-year-old, but the song was too big for you, babe.' Both Perry's and Cole's verdicts had started with praise but ended with a criticism. Cowell, however, had started with a criticism and ended with praise.

How would Louis Walsh react? As a veteran manager of boy bands and a fellow countryman of Niall's, would he offer praise that was more generous? 'No, I think you've got something,' Walsh said. 'I think that people will absolutely like you because you're likeable.' As with many Walsh verdicts, the wording was slightly oddball. Cowell quickly jumped on it, saying sarcastically, 'People will like him because he's likeable?' Walsh told Cowell to 'shut up', much to everyone's amusement, including Niall's. But, for the youngster, the fact he had been given some unequivocal praise was the most important, and pleasing, thing. It gave him some confidence going into the all-important judges' votes.

Sometimes, it is obvious from the feedback each judge

gives as to which way her or his vote will go. But not this time. Cowell went first. 'Well, I'm going to say yes,' he said. Niall was thrilled. Having secured a 'yes' from the hardest to please of the judges, he felt full of confidence. He punched the air like a footballer, then kissed his hand and crossed himself. However, his excitement was quickly deflated when Cole followed with her verdict: it was a 'no'. Little Niall looked absolutely devastated, his eyes showing his hurt and deflation. By the usual sequence, Perry, who was sitting to Cole's right, should have been next to speak but cheeky Walsh jumped the queue and told Niall, 'I'm going to say yes!' The Irishman knew just what he was doing: by jumping in he had made sure that Perry would deliver the casting vote. Knowing the American's tendency to people-please, he was making it harder for her to say no. He was doing what he could to help Niall through to the next round. 'So now,' he explained with trademark excitement, 'he needs three yeses!'

Perry, realizing she was under pressure, mimed a stabbing motion into her own neck, signifying how she felt she had been stitched up to a degree. Cowell, who was sitting at the end of panel, observed all this drama with an admiring grin on his face – he loves a bit of mischief. Perry was less happy and looked as if she was on the brink of sending Niall home. 'Can I just say that I agree with

Cheryl: you do need more experience. And, by the way, just if you're likeable . . . likeableness is not going to sell records. It's talent – and you have a seed of it.' She then paused for a moment, prompting Walsh – who by this stage seemed nearly as anxious as Niall – to plead, 'Go *ooonnnn*!' Perry took one more moment to consider, then said, 'Of course, you're in.'

Niall had done it – but there could be little doubt he had only just squeezed through. He cheered in delight, the microphone picking up a surprisingly deep and manly cheer. As he left the stage, Perry told him, 'Don't let us down.' After he had left the stage triumphantly, the panel continued to discuss him among themselves. 'He's got charm,' said Cowell. 'He's got something.' Although the judges did not view Niall at this stage as anywhere particularly near a finished product, they saw promise and potential in him. It is with these sorts of acts that *The X Factor* makes a mark – the rough diamonds who turn into honed stars under the watchful gaze of Cowell and his crew. In Niall, they had a diamond ripe for polishing. Although Niall had come across as very confident, overconfident in the eyes of some, the judges' guarded praise for him had brought him back to earth. The fact that he reacted to their tempered verdicts with dignity would be useful for him in the eyes of the viewers. On some occasions, auditionees have been tetchy in the face of such critiques. While such reactions make for great television, they only harm the act in question.

As he left the stage, Niall felt a tinge of disappointment that he hadn't received a straight set of positive votes, but he had three out of four, and that was good enough for him. He saw other contestants leaving in floods of tears after they had been roundly rejected by the panel, which put his slight disappointment into perspective. Niall returned to his family and celebrated his progress through to the next round – boot camp, the most ruthless and unpredictable *X Factor* round.

Having watched previous series of the show, Niall knew that the producers loved to spring surprises during boot camp. Contestants are culled without pity and the format and rules change each year to keep contestants on their toes and the viewers interested. In 2010, boot camp would be held at Wembley, with 200 contestants battling it out for a place in the next round of the show – judges' houses. At the start of boot camp, the contestants were gathered on the stage so the judges could address them. Niall was terrified as Walsh told the assembled that half of the contestants were to be sent home on the first day. He realized that he could be one of the rejected half and resolved to give his very best. Walsh's pep talk had worked on Niall.

Each of the four categories – boys, girls, bands and over-twenty-fives – was given a different song to perform. The boys – who included Niall – were handed 'Man in the Mirror' by Michael Jackson. During their breaks, Niall took his guitar outside and sang on the steps, strumming away and leading singalongs with his fellow contestants. Niall led a performance of his favourite Bieber song 'Baby', and in a video shot of the impromptu performance a certain Liam Payne can be seen joining the throng, sitting down behind Niall. The Irish lad's charisma is clear to see in the video, as he gamely leads the rapping part of the song, a point at which many of his fellow contestants had given up. Niall was, as ever, people-pleasing effectively, every inch the cheeky Irish chap.

Overnight, at the hotel, Niall shared a room with future bandmate Liam. They sang songs together, talked about their ambitions and had a laugh. However, Niall noticed how serious and focused Liam was. The Midlander, who had entered *The X Factor* two years before, only to be sent home by Simon Cowell at the judges'-houses phase, was determined to succeed this time. There was an intensity and seriousness about him that seemed slightly chilling at times, and made for an interesting contrast between the two roommates. While Niall was definitely determined and serious about the challenge ahead, his easygoing and s way formed a nice counterbalance to Liam's more uptight and sombre mood. One evening, Niall later recalled, the hotel got 'wrecked'. He insists he played no part in the destruction and says he was fast asleep at the time. He recalls a hazy memory of someone kicking the door of his hotel room at around 2 a.m., the sound waking him up. After returning to sleep, he rose the next morning to find broken glass and other debris on the hotel floor. 'I know who was responsible, but I'm not telling,' he wrote in *Forever Young*. Nevertheless, he had found the hotel experience 'a real laugh'.

The next day, there came the first boot-camp surprise of the series when Cowell told the assembled acts that the judges would not be sending anyone home that day. He also told the hopefuls that he had spotted a star in each of the categories. This was music to Niall's ears, but no sooner had he and the other contestants relaxed than they were told that the task for the day was to be dancing lessons. The flamboyant *X Factor* choreographer Brian Friedman arrived to put them through their paces. Wearing a hooded green jumper, opened to the waist, he looked his usual stark self and approached the tutorial in his trademark no-nonsense style, telling them, 'I don't want you to be scared. What we're going to work on is your stage presence and choreography.' They danced to 'Telephone' by Lady Gaga, and Niall, wearing a purple T-shirt and baggy jeans, did his best to step up to the task in hand. However, dancing has never been his strong point and, while he could hardly be faulted for effort, on technique he was found lacking. 'He's all over the place,' noted Cowell, who was watching with Walsh. Niall was not the only future member of One Direction for whom this was not their finest hour – Zayn Malik went and hid backstage.

At the end of the day, the contestants were given a list of forty songs from which to choose their track to sing the following day. Walsh again ratcheted up the pressure by telling them this was their final chance, so they should be sure not to mess up. Niall chose 'Champagne Supernova' by Oasis, an anthemic song that the band released during their mid-1990s Britpop heyday. Niall had selected it reasoning that nobody else would have chosen it, hoping that, if he was the only one to sing it, he would stand out all the more. His prediction was correct, although future bandmates Liam and Harry both sang another Oasis song, 'Stop Crying Your Heart Out', which is taken from a later album, *Heathen Chemistry*. (Both Gallagher brothers are fans of *The X Factor*, and Noel has been approached to be a judge.)

For this performance, no feedback would be given to the contestants at the time – they would simply sing, then leave the stage. And the other contestants would be sitting behind the judges watching the auditions, which made for an intense experience, as Niall would be facing not just the judges and the cameras, but also his rivals. As he watched his future bandmates perform, Niall was unaware of the fate that lay in store for them. After Liam Payne and Harry Styles had both sung individually their Oasis song, Louis Tomlinson and Zayn Malik both chose to perform Bob Dylan's 'Make You Feel My Love', made famous more recently by the award-winning British songbird Adele. This was the last chance to impress the judges before the final cut would be made.

The nerves among the contestants were palpable. Cowell told them, 'Today will be the most important day of your lives,' before informing them that Nicole Scherzinger would be joining the panel to help cut down the contestants, which Niall was thrilled to hear. He was stunned by how beautiful she was when she walked in, and amused when she told the contestants, 'It's time to separate the men from the boys and the pussycats from the dolls.' The singer had joined the fray because Cheryl Cole had been sent home after collapsing backstage. It was later reported that she had contracted the malaria bug while on holiday in Tanzania. She was taken to hospital and told there would be a lengthy recuperation ahead for her. (There was an eerie irony to this: it made for an unwitting foreshadow of a drama that would erupt on the US version of *The X Factor* the following year, when, after Cole was dropped as a judge, Scherzinger moved in to take her place.)

In a change to previous series, *X Factor* producers decided not to allow an audience to attend the process. The series' official Twitter account sent out the following message: 'Due to the unusual circumstances, we are not inviting an audience to watch the contestants perform at *The X Factor* Boot Camp', which added a dose of drama to what happened next. Niall also learned that instead of the anticipated six contestants from each category going through to the next round, eight would go through. Suddenly, the stakes had changed and Niall felt a renewed rush of confidence. However, as he and the rest of his category stood on the stage, he got a funny feeling that he wasn't going to be chosen.

As they lined up on the stage to discover their fate, the tension was almost too much to bear. As each name was called, Niall's hopes collapsed. It was hard to applaud those who had been put through, as each person who succeeded made it less likely that Niall would make it. He was wearing a black jumper pulled over a shirt and looked adorable. When the final name was called, Niall realized, or believed, that his *X Factor* journey was over. 'That's it, guys', said Cowell, confirming the worst. Niall ruffled his hair as the situation sank in. As he left the stage, a camera crew approached him, eager to capture the drama and heartache on film. Niall did his best to explain how he felt. He was fighting back the tears and ended up turning away from the camera, and pulling his jumper over his face to hide it. He wrote in *Forever Young*, 'That's the worst thing I've ever had happen to me in my life. I was standing there waiting for my name to be called out, and then it wasn't. I was so upset.' As he came to terms with the rejection, he resolved that he would enter again the following year. Perhaps, he hoped, with twelve months' extra experience and work, he could do better in 2011. However, the biggest twist in boot-camp history, perhaps in *The X Factor* itself, was about to throw Niall right back into the mix.

In an instant, he would morph from yet another heartbroken *X Factor* reject to become a leading contender. As he wept backstage, it felt as if his dream was over. However, as he was just about to discover, it would be, as Niall had hoped from the start, game on.

CHAPTER THREE

THE BOYS ARE ALL RIGHT

Suddenly, Niall Horan's *X Factor* experience was steering away from the script he had expected. A producer approached the contestants, among whom Niall was tearfully standing, to make a surprise announcement. They were not sure what was afoot, but they were aware it might be good news. Niall nervously bit his fingernails as he considered what might happen next. Standing right next to him, his future bandmate Louis Tomlinson also chomped at his fingers. Both wore expressions that suggested they were anticipating good, exciting news, while simultaneously trying to hold their expectations in check. It was a tough balancing act to maintain the circumstances; the fact that the camera crew were recording every moment closely only added to the sense that something special was afoot here. Niall was, as he explained on a later ITV2 documentary, packed and ready to go home.

Meanwhile, backstage, Cowell had decided he was not happy to lose Niall and four of the boys. Harry Styles, Liam Payne, Zayn Malik and Louis Tomlinson. 'I had a bad feeling that maybe we shouldn't have lost them and maybe there was something else we should do with them,' he explained later. 'And this is when the idea came about that we should see if they could work as a group.' In truth, there is inevitably a certain amount of mythmaking in the production of a reality series such as *The X Factor*. So it is fair to speculate that a decision to form Niall, Liam, Zayn, Louis and Harry into a band had been taken earlier in the series. The narrative that all four were sent home, only for a sudden decision to be made to bring them back, is convenient and certainly made for good television. A bit of polish and spin is to be expected in any television series – there is nothing sinister to it.

In any case, as the band lined up on the stage, Cowell looked at them and decided he had definitely made the right decision. 'The minute they stood there for the first time together – it was a weird feeling,' he told *Rolling Stone* later. 'They just looked like a group at that point.' It was indeed notable that the five boys seemed to meld effortlessly into a unit. Their charisma and unity was stark. However, unified though they looked, they were also confused. Why had they been called back? It was Scherzinger who kicked off the explanation. 'Hello. Thank you so much for coming back,' she told them. 'Judging from some of your faces, this is really hard. We've thought long and hard about it and we've thought of each of you as individuals and we just feel that you're too talented to let go of. We think it would be a great idea to have two separate groups.' Still, the penny had not completely dropped with the contestants, so Cowell decided to make it clear. 'We've decided to put you both through to the judges' houses,' he told them.

As the two bands celebrated, Cowell interrupted to add a work-based note of caution. He wanted Niall and the others to understand that, though they had a great opportunity ahead of them, they would have to really focus and labour to make it happen. 'Guys, guys, girls, girls, this is a lifeline: you've got to work ten, twelve, fourteen hours a day, every single day, and take this opportunity,' he told them. 'You've got a real shot here, guys.' Cowell is the sort of person who, when he speaks, makes people listen. Nowhere is this more true than within his *X Factor* bubble. The bands absorbed what he had said. 'It was a shock because when I entered

The X Factor, no way did I ever think I was going to end up in a band,' Niall told ITV2 later. Before the line-up could be fully confirmed, Liam wanted to take a bit of time to consider his options. Having built up what he felt was a noteworthy head of steam as a solo singer since his previous *X Factor* experience, he wondered whether he really wanted to join an experimental boy band. He eventually decided he did – and the band was officially an item!

In due course, as Cowell was shown on the series being told which of the categories the producers wanted him to mentor, he feigned annoyance at being given the band category. Previously, this had always been considered one of the less exciting categories to mentor, due in part to the fact that a band had never won *The X Factor*. In reality, in this particular year he was probably thrilled to be in charge of the newly formed boy band's category. He had very high hopes for the band and would delight in being, week by week during the live shows, positioned as the man who brought them together and guided them through. Indeed, once the live shows kicked off, there would be bickering from Walsh and Cowell, both of whom wanted to lay claim to being behind the band's success. It was amusing to watch these elder adults squabbling over their connection to a bunch of teenage boys.

*

Meanwhile, the band needed a name. During a chat, Harry commented that the band were all headed in one direction. And that, or so the story goes, is how the band struck upon that as a name: One Direction. Band legend also has it that Niall had suggested a different name: 'Niall and the Potatoes'. He was only joking, though.

In fact, Niall was the focus of one of the newly formed band's first discussions. Liam recalled that chat. The band stood in a circle and talked about their future. One of the first things they wanted to consider was their look. The other four members noticed that Niall was wearing cool shoes. 'We were, like, "Let's dress like Niall,"' said Liam. 'That was the first conversation we had.' Then the band had to consider where they would congregate for get-togethers prior to the judges'-houses phase. The fact that Niall came from Ireland was the biggest complication, but the band quickly settled on Harry's family home at Holmes Chapel in Cheshire as the best place to assemble. There was a bungalow at the foot of the garden which was just big enough to house five excitable teenage boys. Then there was the garden space itself, which included an outdoor pool.

This was teenage-boy heaven. There followed some hugely enjoyable days in which the boys mucked about, rehearsed, got to know each other and slowly bonded. Zayn, who was the last to arrive, took a little longer to settle in with the band. When they sang, it was Niall who, as well as singing, provided the backing track, strumming his guitar. When they got hungry they clubbed together and piled into a car, which Louis, the eldest member of One Direction, would drive to a local fast-food outlet.

These would, in retrospect, be hugely important and valuable days for Niall and the band. They were able to live their days the way they wanted to, before *The X Factor* machine and then the pop industry itself would begin to dictate just about their every move. Amid the fun there was also a certain amount of chaos. The bungalow became more and more messy. One day a chair was broken. 'It all got a bit rock-and-roll,' said Harry's mother Anne, during a later interview with Radio 1. 'Boys will be boys.' Another feature of the week was Harry's tendency to get naked at the drop of a hat. Niall got an eyeful of Harry's naked body on several occasions, thanks to Harry's belief that being naked was 'liberating' and beneficial to 'confidence'.. Louis, meanwhile, said in *Celebs on Sunday* magazine that one morning Harry woke him from his sleep by hitting him 'round the head with his penis – it actually wrapped around my whole face'. This is an image that will either delight or disgust the reader, but a cheeky scamp was what Harry was proving to be. One day, Niall was quietly sitting on the toilet, the door of which he had, unfortunately, left unlocked. 'Harry burst in and took a picture of me,' Niall remembered later. 'Two weeks later for my birthday, I got a present from him and it was a mug with a picture of me on the toilet on it. You have to pour hot water in and then the picture shows up.' However, the sarcastic gift was not long for this world. 'I broke the handle off it,' Niall admitted. His bandmate Liam said, with mock disgust, 'He broke it! We got him a nice present and he broke it.'

After the fun, it was time to work. The newly christened band flew to the villa Simon Cowell had rented on the Costa Del Sol in Marbella for the judges'-houses round. Niall had been so excited as he set off, and his excitement only built when he saw the property they would be staying in: it was a magnificent place. The boys thought they had tasted luxury at Harry's home but this was on an entirely different scale. The mansion had twenty bedrooms, three vast swimming pools, a gym and a luxurious cinema. No wonder it cost £15,000 per week to hire for the show! There, they would absolutely sail through to the next round. Speaking later to *Rolling Stone* magazine about the band's history, Cowell was asked when he first realized that the band could be huge. 'When they came to my house in Spain and performed, after about a millionth of a second,' he said. 'I tried to keep a straight face for a bit of drama for the show.' There was drama behind the scenes, too. Louis was bitten by a sea urchin and wild parties were held by the contestants.

Indeed, when they arrived they committed the sin of waking up Cowell, who was keeping strange hours, as is his wont. There were also reports that the bands' parties had led to damage to the property. 'Yes, they did wake me up,' Cowell told reporters. 'To teach them a lesson, any damage to the villa will have to be paid out their first royalty cheque – if they make it.' The band also picked up on some resentment from other bands in the category. There was a feeling among some that, as Cowell had been instrumental in forming One Direction, they would have an unfair advantage. Such tensions and suspicions are all part of a contest like *The X Factor* – putting a bunch of ambitious and creative types together and charging them to compete with one another is always going to create tension.

It had been touch and go as to whether Louis would be able to sing on the big day owing to his urchin bite, but he managed to make it at the last moment, albeit with a rather swollen foot. Niall stood at the right-hand end of the line-up. Liam led the vocals during the first verse, Harry took the bridge and then all five, including Niall, sang during the chorus. Niall turned in to face the band as they swung their hips during the final chorus. The band looked convincing as a unit, particularly considering the tender age of both the band and its individuals.

At the end of the song, Cowell gave nothing away to the band, merely saying, 'See you later.' However, as the boys filed away from the audition, Niall high-fiving the resident guitarist, Chris Leonard, Cowell was struggling to contain his enthusiasm. He and his aide Sinitta both expressed their excitement over what they had seen. 'They're cool, they're relevant,' said Cowell. In an article in *Rolling Stone* in April 2012, he expanded on how he felt at that moment. 'The second they left I jumped out of my chair,' he recalled. 'They just had it. They had this confidence. They were fun. They worked out the arrangements themselves. They were like a gang of friends, and kind of fearless as well.' There would be little soul-searching needed when he decided whether to put One Direction through to the live shows.

Still, when it came to breaking the news to them the following day, Cowell naturally played it as deadpan as he could while building their and the viewers' suspense. 'My head is saying it's a risk and my heart is saying that you deserve a shot,' he told them. 'And that's why it's been difficult. So I've made a decision. Guys, I've gone with my heart – you're through!'

The roar that came from the boys as they celebrated said it all. They then ran to celebrate with Cowell – Harry the first to arrive in the arms of their mentor, but Niall not far behind him. 'I am so impressed with all of you; I mean that,' Cowell told them. Then they ran off and jumped into the nearby swimming pool. All of them, that is, apart from the injured Louis.

Then they headed back to Britain. It was a flight of conflicting emotions for Niall: on the one hand he was overjoyed to have progressed, yet he felt obliged to camouflage his excitement so as to not offend those acts who had been less lucky. On arrival in London, they had the exciting challenge of the live shows ahead as they pitted themselves against the other finalists in a bid to win the public vote and be crowned *X Factor* champions.

First, Niall and the band spent a few nights in hotels while the contestants' house was made ready. When they arrived at the house, they were so excited, and with good reason: the £3.5 million Spanish-style mansion, set on a private road in Borehamwood, Hertfordshire, was grand indeed. The road was surrounded by thick woods. The reported weekly rent for the property was £50,000, but the producers felt it was well worth it after their experiences in the previous series. Then, they had rented a house in north London that had become besieged by fans and bored kids from schools who formed quite a throng, surrounding the house making noise at all hours of the day and night. They also plastered its walls with graffiti, some of it lewd. Local residents, among which were the Chinese ambassador, were not impressed. However, private security guards were booked to patrol the Hertfordshire property where Niall and his fellow finalists stayed.

Naturally, they quickly made the sort of mess of which only teenage boys are capable. Members of the girl band Belle Amie were horrified by the smell and sight of the band's room, so they tidied it. The adjoining bathroom was also messy, with abandoned orange-juice cartons joining worn underwear on the floor and other surfaces. Although Louis was ranked as the least tidy of the five boys, Niall had his part to play in the mayhem. Cowell was fairly laid back about the mess, however, arguing that it is important to allow the finalists to 'be their age and do what they like'. He added, in the *Daily Mail*, 'They are entering the music business for all the right reasons, and that is not to sit in the library till three in the morning.' There was little danger of that!

Niall had a memorable experience in the aforementioned bathroom one evening. Again it involved his bandmate Harry interrupting him – but for more serious reasons this time – as Niall performed what is usually a somewhat private function. After eating dinner, Niall had retired to the toilet. As he recalled in *X Magazine* in October 2010, 'He ran into the toilet but I was doing a poo at the time. He's shouting at me, "Get out the way, get out the way," but I can't move because I'm on the loo.' Harry ended up with no choice but to vomit explosively into the bath, while the excreting Niall looked on with a blend of horror and embarrassment. 'It turned out he burst blood vessels in his neck,' said Niall. 'He'd got food poisoning.' Harry was soon rushed off to see a doctor, while Niall completed his formalities.

Niall also described another of Harry's less ideal moments in the house. This time, it involved – let's be thankful for small mercies – the kitchen rather than the bathroom. 'He almost burned the house down the other day,' Niall said. 'He was cooking pizzas and burnt them to a crisp. But we ate them anyway because we hate wasting food.' That final line was straight out of a public-relations text book – Niall was learning fast how to say the right things.

They spent many fun hours in what they called 'the beanbag room', playing computer games and table tennis. Sometimes the finalists would gather in the beanbag room and sing as a chorus, while Matt Cardle (who would go on to become the 2010 winner of *The X Factor*) strummed his guitar. Niall, the guitarist for pre-live show get-togethers, allowed the older Cardle to pull rank for the time being.

Some of the boys felt homesick at times, but not Niall. He sees time spent away from home as a time for fun and adventure, and time to build up fresh affection for those he's been parted from. That said, his parents travelled over for the live shows whenever they could They were so proud and excited. They felt anxiety, too, particularly as, each week, the results of the public vote were announced.

For Niall, the weeks ahead would conform to a similar schedule. Each Sunday, the acts would begin work on their song(s) for the following weekend's show. The preparation would continue into Monday, during which the list would be honed. During Tuesday, the dancing and choreography for the performance would be rehearsed with Brian Friedman putting them through their paces. The American admitted that he found working with the band challenging, due to their cheeky and misbehaving ways. He said trying to maintain order during their sessions kept him young. 'One Direction? It's every direction except where I need them to be!' During Thursday and Friday the band would continue to rehearse their song at the Wembley studios. There, they would be met by an increasingly large group of fans who hung around outside. 'More and more people were starting to build outside the studios,' recalled Niall on ITV2.

In Week One, Niall was delighted when he learned that the band would be performing his favourite song, 'Viva La Vida' by Coldplay. It was a surprising song for a boy band to kick off their campaign with. As such, is was a shrewd choice. It sent out a strong message that this was not to be a stereotypical boy band, sitting on stools and then rising in the key change of yet another soppy ballad. Nor would they be signing an R&B boy-band song of the type favoured by the Wanted and *X Factor* graduates JLS.

Instead, the band would be a little more adventurous. Niall and the boys put an enormous effort and lots of time into preparing for their debut live show performance. They were also visited by stylists who had been tasked with giving them a major makeover. For Niall, this was a particularly tricky experience. He was familiar with hair colouring, as he had been adding blond highlights to his brown locks for some time. However, for the makeover he was given an entirely beached-blond head of hair. 'I'm not going to lie, it hurt my scalp,' he wrote in *Forever Young*. 'I didn't know how women do it.' The style his hair was worked into for the band footage to be used in the VTs showed him with an uncomfortable and ill-judged style, which was quickly dumped for a more messy and familiar look.

As they prepared for the performance, they were all very nervous, Harry so much so that he was sick backstage. Zayn, meanwhile, was terrified that he would miss his cue. As for Niall, he managed to keep his nerves more or less under control. His easygoing nature really came to the fore at times such as these. Wearing a dark T-shirt and grey trousers with high-top shoes, he took his place at the right-hand end of the band, next to Louis. He looked the most relaxed of the group, his wide smile and calm body language contrasting with Harry's look of nervous aggression. If there could be one criticism levelled at Niall this week, it would be that he was perhaps too happy. When it came to his turn to sing, his bright smile sat ill at ease with the regretful lyric he was singing. However, this is nit-picking with the benefit of hindsight. On the night, Niall's beaming happiness was enjoyable. Even his regular, somewhat awkward, pulling up of his trousers was cute.

Near the end of the performance, Liam beckoned Niall to up his game. The Midlander had noted that the delivery was fading slightly. Niall responded well. The band had done themselves justice. Niall stood with a combination of relief and pride as the song ended and the audience screamed their admiration. Then it was time for the judges' verdicts. Walsh was the first to speak. 'Wow, guys, when I heard you were going to do Coldplay, I thought it was a big, big risk! I love what you did with the song – you totally made it your own. I love that the band is gelling. Even though Simon's going to claim he put this band together, it was my idea originally, Simon. It was! Boys, I think potentially you could be the next big boy band, but you have a lot of work to do.' There was a string in the tail. He added, 'But, Simon Cowell, I'm not sure about the styling! Did you have a stylist?' As the audience weighed in with plentiful pantomime booing,

Walsh hardened his face and jutted out his chin in defiance.

Dannii Minogue, ever the serious judge rather than clowning character, avoided the bickering and focused on the performance itself. 'Guys, I don't know whose idea it was because I wasn't there, but you look like you fit together, you're the perfect band,' she said. The boys were thrilled with the feedback and they congratulated one another. 'That song was fantastic and you did make it your own,' added the Australian.

Cheryl Cole felt much the same. 'I have to agree with Dannii: you look like you were meant to be together as a group,' she said. The boys were thrilled to be praised by such a beautiful woman – and there was even better to come. 'I reckon the girls will be going crazy for you, but you need a little bit more time to develop as a group, that's all,' she added. 'Just a little bit more time.'

Cowell, their mentor, then spoke. Predictably, he had things to say about what Walsh had just said. 'Regarding your role in putting the group together, Louis, we'll rewind the tapes on that one,' he said. Walsh suggested that, yes, he should. 'You guys came together because your boot-camp auditions weren't good enough but you were too good to throw away,' Cowell continued. 'We took a risk, and I've got to tell you, what was so impressive about that was when you started to screw up: one of you at the end, Liam, stepped in, you brought it back together. That's what bands do.' He then turned to Walsh's comments regarding styling: 'Louis, I don't want to style a band like this. We asked the band to do whatever they wanted to do. I'm not going to interfere. They're going to do it their way. It was brilliant, guys.'

The presenter, the ever chipper Dermot O'Leary, then joined the conversation, saying, 'Louis, with the greatest respect, how do you know what eighteen-year-olds should be wearing? Come on, man!'

Niall was most amused by the judges' banter. It reminded him of Walsh and Cowell's verbal jousting at his first audition. He was also enjoying the solidity he and his fellow band members were feeling. 'Surprisingly, considering how long we'd known each other, we were already like five brothers,' he wrote in *Forever Young*. 'I know it's a bit of a cliché, but it's true.'

The following evening, a verdict even more important than that of the judges would arrive, in the shape of the results of the public vote. Niall was worried about the outcome. While they had a growing fanbase, screams aplenty in the live studio and fine feedback from the judges, if the public were not enamoured of the band, it would be a quick one-way ticket back to normality for Niall and the other four. This would be the most nervous he and the band would feel throughout the series.

But, to their joy, they survived the vote to go through to the next week. Niall jumped up and down, spinning round in circles of celebration. Less lucky was solo singer Nicolò Festa, who exited automatically after finishing at the bottom of the voting pile, and the band FYD, who lost the sing-off with controversial crooner Katie Waissel. Cowell, meanwhile, had noted that One Direction were quickly attracting substantial gaggles of fans outside the studio. 'It was unusual because in an instant we had hundreds of fans outside the studio,' he told *Rolling Stone* later. 'That doesn't happen very often.'

Backstage, the band were building their relationship with mentor Cowell. He welcomed, almost encouraged, their irreverent and cheeky ways with him. They dubbed him 'Uncle Simon', which would have pricked the ever-vain Cowell's ego slightly, though not as much as his being dubbed a father figure would have done. He was celebrating his fifty-first birthday during the week of the first live show. He could not help but giggle when he opened his birthday card from Niall's band, as inside it was £2.50 in cash. Each band member had donated 50 pence. In no time at all, One Direction would be making Cowell a fortune, of course.

Perhaps suitably, then, for the second week of the live shows, the theme was 'heroes'. At this stage, fourteen acts remained in the reckoning. Amid the excitement and hope, there was still a long way for Niall and the group to go. The One Direction song choice for the week was the pop anthem 'My Life Would Suck Without You', by Kelly Clarkson. In a sense, there was a nice symbolism behind the song choice: Clarkson, the winner of the first ever series of *American Idol*, is one of the most successful figures in television talent-show history, and therefore was a fine example for Niall to look up to at this stage in the process. That said, as a female solo artist's song, it was a second successive unlikely choice. One Direction were clearly being steered away from boy band clichés in this early stage of their career. It would have been easy to give them ballads, or even more urban boy-band tracks, such as those of the Wanted, or *X Factor* graduates JLS. Instead, they were being handed imaginative song choices and seemed all the fresher for it.

During rehearsals in Week Two, Harry was once more hit by an attack of nerves. Niall gave him a protective, reassuring cuddle, providing an early hint of the calming, protective influence he would have within One Direction. Indeed, each of the band members was developing a distinct identity within the unit. Liam was becoming 'the serious one', though Louis could, on occasion, rival him for that role. Harry was the band's charmer, with Zayn the quiet one, though not to the degree that outsiders believed.

Niall was described by Liam as someone who 'just wants to have a laugh twenty-four/seven'. Louis said that Niall had a terrible memory – 'he's like a goldfish'. However, all of these identities were fluid, and at any given point Niall, say, could become serious, with Liam suddenly playing the clown. It made for a refreshing unit. Though they had the odd brief bicker, at this stage the band were gelling and getting on. At heart, they were four teenage lads like any others – but for the fact that they were starring in a major talent show in front of millions of viewers each weekend.

When it came to Saturday evening, the band performed 'My Life Would Suck Without You' rather well. The band were moodily lit for the opening segment. As Liam took the opening verse the camera panned between the others. It immediately showed Niall and Louis grinning again, while Harry was again jutting along to the music. Niall continued to be impish, trading cheeky smiles with his immediate neighbour, Zayn, and the audience. His unbridled joy at being there was palpable. If his enthusiasm at times seemed a little too strong, few would not forgive him his bubbliness.

It was, overall, a good performance, with only a bum note from Zayn detracting slightly from the perfection. Walsh was, again, the first to give feedback. Once more, he took the opportunity to include a playful dig at Cowell. 'Well, One Direction, you seem to be having fun on stage,' he said. 'Every schoolgirl up and down the country is going to love this. My only problem, boys, is with your mentor Simon. Kelly Clarkson a hero? Simon, why? It was a strange song. Boys, you are really, really good but I think Simon Cowell could've picked a better song.' Again, he was booed by One Direction's admirers in the audience.

Minogue, turned the talk to more pertinent terrain. She said, 'Boys, maybe that's your musical hero. I have to say that you're five heartthrobs.' Niall pumped his fist in celebration at this comment. 'You look great together. And, Harry, whatever nerves you have, I'm sure your friends and you will stick together. The true measure of a boy band like you will be when you sing your big ballad, so I'll be looking forward to hearing that.'

When Cole spoke, she uttered the sort of words that most teenage boys would dream of hearing from her lips. 'I can't even cope with how cute you are,' she said. 'Seriously, I can't!' Niall was thrilled, as Cole had long been his ultimate celebrity crush, and Harry put his hands together as if offering a prayer of thanks to the heavens. 'I just want to go over and hug them, in a nice way. You're so sweet. I'm watching you the whole time just thinking, "This is adorable."'

As Cole had said all this, Cowell had theatrically, and humorously, warned her off the boys, saying, 'No, no, no!'

When it came to his own time to comment, he offered the band some colossal praise, even surpassing his sycophancy of the previous week. 'Let me tell you, you are the most exciting pop band in the country today,' he told the boys, much to their stunned disbelief. 'I'm being serious – there is something absolutely right.'

Exciting times for One Direction – and, to their increased excitement the following evening, Niall and his bandmates were once again voted through.

In Week Three, the theme was 'guilty pleasures'. Niall's band sang the Pink song, 'Nobody Knows'. To inject some melodrama into proceedings, the producers filmed Cowell deciding, late in the week, to change the band's song for the weekend. This was treated as a plot twist of approaching apocalyptic gravity, and a challenge of almost epic proportion. Niall and the lads managed to step up the challenge and deliver another fine performance.

Afterwards, the judges continued their now weekly contest to see who could deliver the most fawning and hyperbolic comment. Walsh began by comparing them to the Canadian king of pop. 'You just have to walk out on the stage. Everybody's screaming,' said the Irishman, noting the excited noise filling the venue. 'It's like five Justin Biebers! And Liam – brilliant lead vocal from you!'

Minogue, comparatively more measured but still utterly admiring, observed that they were 'living the dream'.

Cole said, with a cheeky smile, 'You know what, guys? Let me just put this out there: you are my guilty pleasure!' That was just the start of it, though. She then won the weekly hyperbole contestant as she added, 'Whenever the Beatles went anywhere, they caused that level of hysteria.' This was an astonishing comparison to make. Niall had been compared to Bieber even before his *X Factor* experience began; it was a comparison he enjoyed implicitly making himself. Yet he had surely never been compared to the Fab Four before. 'You're finding your feet now, I'm looking forward to seeing you improve even more.'

Their mentor Cowell was his usual proud self. Having once more milked the whole song-change issue all he could, he said, 'I've got to tell you, apart from it being a great performance, I thought, vocally, you've really, really made some really huge improvements.'

The audience agreed with the judges and once again voted the boys through.

The comparison with the Beatles may have shocked Niall, but during the week ahead he had a fright of another kind when he and the band visited the London Dungeon ahead of the following weekend's Hallowe'en-themed show. The

London Dungeon is a tourist attraction aimed mainly at a younger audience, and features actors and special effects to recreate macabre events in history. Zayn said on *The X Factor* that the experience was 'a real laugh', and mocked Niall, who 'got scared' by what they saw there. 'It was pretty scary, like,' said Niall in his defence.

They also went to north London's Koko venue to see a Tinie Tempah concert. Here, it was Liam's turn for discomfort. When Tempah invited the band up onto the stage, Liam slipped over and twisted his ankle. Later, they found themselves in the VIP booth with Girls Aloud stars Nicola Roberts and Kimberley Walsh, as well as the male solo star Chipmunk.

The London Dungeon, though, had been the truly blood-curdling experience and set the mood for the Hallowe'en show ahead. There, they would be styled right up to the ghostly hilt, and would finally sing a song that was associated in the public mind with boy bands. There had, in fact, been some concern over the song choice, which was 'Total Eclipse of the Heart', originally sung by Bonnie Tyler but, more recently, it had been covered by the Irish boy band Westlife, and was thus considered a boy-band song by the younger generation, many of whom would have been unaware of Tyler's gravelly voice (her recording had been way back in 1983). Walsh, for instance, had been concerned about the song and others involved with the show also expressed anxiety.

When it came to their performance, the boys appeared with ghoulish makeup on. Niall opened the vocals, with a moody 'Turn around . . .' Although it was Niall and Liam who took most of the lead vocal parts this week, it was notable that Harry had moved into the centre of the line-up. The gradual 'changing of the guard' from Liam to Harry as the band's unofficial leader was under way.

'I love the whole *Twilight*, vampire thing going on in the background,' said Walsh, leading the feedback. 'Simon, it's definitely working.'

Minogue added: 'You make vampire hot – I want to come to your party!'

Cole, too, spoke with excitement at the band's commercial potential: 'It doesn't matter where I go, somebody – an older woman, young women, kids, everybody – mentions One Direction. I think you have a really long way to go in this competition.'

Cowell summed up the mood: 'What I really admire about you guys is I know people are under pressure when you go into a competition like this. You've got to remember you're sixteen, seventeen years old. The way you've conducted yourselves – don't believe the hype, work hard, rehearse. Honestly, it's a total pleasure working with you lot.'

There was, though, a slight shadow cast over the evening. Walsh suggested at one stage that Cowell was prioritizing Niall's band over another act in his category, Belle Amie. Backstage, One Direction felt that Walsh's comment was unfair, as it seemed to cast the band as villains. They also worried that it detracted from how hard they were working. The voting public did not seem to mind, however. They voted the band through again, prompting yet another football-style celebration from Niall. Life felt good.

However, the perception that One Direction were the favourites was hard to shift. Belle Amie, the purported key victims of Cowell's alleged preferences, complained during an interview with Viking FM. Band member Sophie Wardman said that if the boy band took to the stage dressed in bin liners to sing 'Baa Baa Black Sheep', they would still get voted through 'with flying colours'. She said, 'I think it's just a lot easier for them.' Similarly, after the camp two-piece act Diva Fever were voted off, member Craig Saggers told the press that Cowell was uninterested in any act other than One Direction. 'He sees pound signs when he looks at them.'

He did – and this metaphorical hallucination was right on the money, as it were.

*

The evolution of the One Direction's unofficial hierarchy seemed to have begun to show only at this stage, but it had been planned behind the scenes for some time. Cowell told *The Xtra Factor* – *The X Factor*'s companion show – that he felt from the start that Harry had something special and charismatic about him. 'I would say you're drawn to Harry's personality,' he said. 'He's very charming and seems to be the one person who would be easiest to talk to.' Given that, in a previous episode of the spin-off show, Cowell had declared that Liam 'bored the pants off me', the fact that Harry was gradually eased into the de facto frontman role is less surprising. Cowell would insist that the member with the most X factor should be at the centre of the band. Niall was on the margins of the line-up at this stage. How things would change! Backstage, *X Factor* staff were full of admiration for the way the band were coming together. Yvie Burnett, the vocal coach who had been involved with the show for several seasons, told the *Daily Record*, 'They look like stars and act like stars – they have got absolutely everything.'

For many observers, the high point of their live-show campaign came when One Direction sang Kim Wilde's track 'Kids in America'. Although there were several weeks of performance to come from them, during which they would continue to astound and impress many viewers, there was something about their rendition of the Wilde song that smacked of authority and arrival. The band were full of energy and cohesion. Harry jumped in the air as the song neared its close, landing with a stamp on the ground to coincide with its final note. All of the boys, including Niall, were carrying themselves with more confidence each week. They were a million miles from the nervous lads who had sung 'Viva La Vida' just a few weeks earlier.

The studio audience's reaction was getting louder each week, too. Walsh picked up on the growing excitement in his feedback on the night: 'Listen, everywhere I go there's hysteria; it's building on this band. You remind me a bit of Westlife, Take That, Boyzone . . . you could be the next big band.'

Minogue stepped out of the aforementioned hysteria to offer a more considered judgement. 'I don't think, vocally, it was the best of the night but a great performance,' she said.

Cole told the boys, 'That absolutely cheered me up and brightened up my night. I thoroughly enjoyed that performance. You are great kids. I love chatting to you backstage. You are just good lads, nice lads.'

Then proud old Uncle Simon told his five 'nephews', 'That was without question your best performance by a mile.'

Things were getting better and better for Niall and his

new pals. During another between-shows week, the band travelled to see the premiere of *Harry Potter and the Deathly Hallows – Part 1*. Niall, who often measured their burgeoning fame by how many already-famous people knew of them, was blown away when he realized that the eponymous star of the Potter franchise, Daniel Radcliffe, knew who the band were. 'It was amazing,' Niall wrote in *Forever Young*. 'He said to us, "It's quite weirdly thrilling for me to meet you all because I have been watching you every week!" We were like, "Daniel Radcliffe watches us!"' They were also thrilled to meet the glamorous Emma Watson, who played Hermione Granger in the films. 'She was so sweet,' he wrote. She told the band they were gentlemen.

In Elton John Week, they sang the ballad 'Something About the Way You Look Tonight'. Walsh told the lads, 'Well, boys, after that performance I think you're only going in one direction, and that direction is the final. I talked to you guys a lot yesterday and I really got to know you. I know that you're taking the whole thing really, really serious and, you know, you're going to be the next big boy band.'

Minogue added, 'Guys, you are so consistent, it's scary!'

Cole, hearing the huge and frenzied cheer from the studio audience, said, 'Listen to that! That's what it's all about: to hear that is the measure of what you've become.'

Cowell said, 'Guys, I want to say something, OK? This is the first time in all the years of *X Factor* where I genuinely believe a group are going to win this competition.' He then reflected on their courteous and professional personalities, before concluding, 'Guys, congratulations.'

Meanwhile, the One Direction frenzy was spreading far beyond *The X Factor*'s borders. Before the series had even finished, it was as if Niall's band had already risen above *The X Factor* to develop an identity in their own right. Some *X Factor* acts struggle to manage this even years after their 'graduation'. But One Direction had caught the imagination of many in the entertainment industry, including Niall's fellow musical Irishmen Westlife. 'They're the whole package,' said Westlife star Shane Filan during a chat with *X Magazine*. 'They're good singers, they're good-looking lads and they're quite cool. They're like a band of Justin Biebers and they've got everything the girls will love.'

Meanwhile, during their between-shows activity the band visited Wembley Stadium to watch the England soccer side take on France in a friendly. Liverpool captain Steven Gerrard met the band and told them that his wife and children were fans of One Direction. He told them to keep going, and gave Niall, who was wearing an England shirt, an encouraging pat. They received expert praise and encouragement from public-relations guru Mark

Borkowski, who told *Star* magazine, 'One Direction are going to be big. They are all good-looking, have got a bit of an attitude and have a fantastic Svengali behind them in Simon Cowell.' Borkowski, who is an internationally known lecturer and speaker on the art of publicity, predicted, 'They'll definitely be millionaires by this time next year. With the right management and material, they've got everything going for them . . . It's all there for them.'

In Week Seven of *The X Factor* 2010, the boys of One Direction tackled the Beatles. Cowell felt it was the 'perfect' theme for the band. He noted a peak in excitement among the band at the prospect. In the pre-performance VT, Cowell's rival judges tried to build some pressure on the band. The man himself, though, was in no doubt that his boys would deliver. 'Can they shine? One hundred million per cent,' said Cowell, never one to sit on the fence.

They performed on a raised platform, singing an alternative-tempo rendition of 'All You Need Is Love'. Niall sang the first half of the second verse and smiled his way through the backing vocals he performed elsewhere in the song. That smile would drop as one of the judges gave the verdict.

The audience reaction was, somehow, even louder than it had been in previous weeks.

'Thank God for you guys,' said Walsh, adding that 'it is good to see the Fab Five singing the Fab Four' and that he believed they were 'in it for the long haul – yes!'

Minogue, though, sounded a note of criticism. 'I've always given you good comments,' she began, 'I just have to say tonight, you guys [Zayn and Niall] were struggling. I don't know if it was caught on-camera, but you were struggling with the backing vocals. Don't let the other guys down. You have to work as a group.'

Naturally, the audience loudly booed. Niall looked a little shocked at Minogue's critique, but did his best to look humble. The same could be said for Zayn's reaction, though Harry looked a little sceptical of Minogue's stance.

Cole, though essentially positive about the performance, did detract from the positivity by complaining about the raised platform they had sung on.

Cowell, when it came to his turn, spoke in competitive tones. Gesturing to his three fellow judges, he said, 'This lot do not want you to do well in the competition. I do – please vote!'

Minogue's feedback had been a milestone in the band's history. It was the first time a judge had strongly turned on them. Afterwards, Niall took Minogue's criticism on the chin. '[She] gave us a bad comment but we're going to get bad comments,' he said. 'So we've got to take it on board and improve it next week.'

Niall showed that the cocky lad who auditioned in Dublin was already maturing into a more considered and poised personality.

Meanwhile, Niall was tasting further experiences of tabloid chatter each week. During this time, rumours surfaced that he and Belle Amie member Sophia were an item. Niall denied the rumour. He was not the only band member to face such speculation: Zayn and Liam had both, at different times, been linked with finalist Cher Lloyd. Meanwhile, solo singer Matt Cardle had reacted furiously to suggestions he was dating Katie Waissel. It was all part of the circus that is erected around *The X Factor*, to the delight of the management, who see pound signs in every column inch.

In the following week, the band visited HMV, where they saw on sale the charity single they had recorded with the other finalists. Niall gleefully bought a copy of the song, which was raising funds for Help for Heroes. They had recorded 'Heroes', the iconic David Bowie track, alongside the other key finalists. Niall was humbled by the experience of meeting staff from the charity. The finalists asked questions about the charity's work and were moved by what they heard. 'It really puts things into perspective,' Niall told the *Sun*. 'We all complained about having to get up early and do this video shoot this morning – I feel so bad about that now. You don't realize how lucky you are. We're doing a huge TV show and other people have really, really tough jobs.'

For Rock Week, they first sang 'Summer of '69', which had been chosen as a song for them by Harry. Louis Walsh told them, 'Hey, boys, it absolutely worked! I love the choice of song, I love the vibe, the vitality you bring to the competition. The competition would not be the same without One Direction.'

Minogue was more positive than the previous week, saying, 'You've clearly done lots of work and really stepped it up. I like that.'

Cole was stunned by the audience hysteria, saying, 'We've got feet stamps going on, there's electricity in the room, it's fantastic.'

However, it was Cowell whose comments were most significant. 'I had nothing to do with this song choice – Harry chose the song, great choice of song,' he said. As Harry beamed his winning smile, he was congratulated by his bandmates, with Niall even toying with Harry's famous curly locks.

However, cheers from the audience and admiring love-ins among the judges were not enough. Cowell then reminded the boys – but in reality his comments were directed firmly at the audience – that they had 'worked your butts off to get where you've got to' and implored the audience once more to 'Please – pick up the phone!'

Then they sang 'You Are So Beautiful to Me' by Joe Cocker. Walsh questioned whether the track qualified as a 'rock song'. Minogue told them their performance was 'stunning'. Cowell said it was 'in some ways my favourite performance from you'. Walsh told them that the song had proved that they were 'a great vocal group – everyone in this group can sing'. Minogue told them they were 'stunning' and Cole added that she felt they had 'a really bright future'. Cowell told them that 'in many ways that was my favourite performance from you', and singled out Zayn for praise.

In the intervening week, they attended the premiere of *The Chronicles of Narnia: The Voyage of the Dawn Treader*. 'It was amazing because it was the perfect set for a *Narnia* film because it started to snow outside,' said Niall on *The X Factor*. They had met the previous year's *X Factor* winner Joe McElderry on the red carpet. For Niall this was a symbolic moment: he had entered the show after watching McElderry's successful journey the previous year, and now here he was meeting the reigning champion on the red carpet. As the band joked, owing to the absence through illness of their mentor Cowell, it had been nice to get some tips from the singer.

For their first song at the semifinal, the boys sang a reworked version of 'Only Girl (in the World)'. An excited Walsh told them, 'Week after week, you're getting better and better, and you bring hysteria to the show. If there is any justice you will absolutely be in the final – you deserve to be in the final.'

Minogue, again, took her comments beyond mere buttering-up. 'Guys, I hope you never let us down because I really wanna see you guys as the next big boy band. I have to say, some weeks you come out and I think it's very samey. That one was brilliant – you really stepped it up for the semifinals.'

Cole then spoke of her part in the band's week, during which she had effectively stood in for Cowell, who had been absent. 'This week, for me, I got to know you all a little bit better because your mentor wasn't here,' she said. However, there was a sting in the tail ahead. 'I thoroughly enjoyed mentoring you . . . but that song for me was a little bit dangerous because it's so current right now as Rihanna's record that you have to completely make it like it was never, ever written for her, and I don't know if it quite worked for me; but I don't think it makes a difference. I hope to see you in the final.'

Cowell quickly closed down Cole's sentiments when it came to his turn to speak. 'Someone's being tactical!' he said in reference to what she had said. He then put into perspective their plight. Noting the huge increase in their stature, he felt moved to remind the viewers that the band would still need public votes. 'I've got to tell you guys, I know this is going to sound a bit biased but I thought this song was absolutely perfect for you because it is exactly what I liked about them – they didn't take the safe option. They chose something completely different; they had the guts to do it . . . Can I just say, you hear all the applause and people at home might think you're safe, but nobody is safe in this competition, and I would urge anyone, please, if they want to see these boys in the final, please pick up the phone and vote for them because they deserve it.'

In the chat with O'Leary that followed, the host again made a joke about the absence of Cowell. Had the band been able to improve, he asked them cheekily, 'because Simon wasn't around this week?' Niall showed his skills of diplomacy in his reply. 'You know, Simon's been great to us,' he said. 'But we're just so grateful for the people who are voting for us.' To show he could be cheeky as well as polished, he then looked towards Cowell and mimed a wiping of his nose.

For their second song on the night, 'Chasing Cars', Niall wore a white shirt, which gave him an even more angelic look than usual. The song had an added intensity, as all concerned were only too aware that it could be their final performance. The judges certainly gave them a rousing reception. 'Liam, Zayn, Niall, Harry and Louis, I know your names! If there's any justice, all the young kids will pick up their phones and they're going to vote One Direction – 'cos you deserve it!' Minogue added, 'Guys, you've got through a really tough week and that was such a classy, classy performance! You've just grown up in front of our eyes . . .'

Cole, again took a tactical angle, saying, 'I know me personally, all the crew, all the staff . . . everybody has grown so found of you guys over the last few weeks,' she said. This almost sounded like a tribute in expectation of their leaving the competition. However, the next part of her feedback imagined a future for the band on the show. 'This week I was so impressed. You didn't have Zayn [who wasn't there due to a bereavement], Simon wasn't around. You showed a real level of maturity and you really deserve a place in the final.'

Cowell added, 'Guys, Tim Byrne, who's been working with you all week, told me that you made a decision this morning to get in at eight in the morning so you could give yourselves more rehearsal time, and that's what it's all about. It's not about excuses: it's about having that great work ethic, picking yourselves up after what was a very tough week. And I said this before – I genuinely mean this – I am proud of you as people as much as I am artists.

That was a great performance – good for you.'

It was a well-pitched comment. A sense had been building up that the boys were being cosseted owing to their connection with King Simon, and also to the fact that the show had effectively formed them. Cowell's comments about their work rate gave the lie to that notion.

In the week leading up to the big final, the show took on an almost election-like feel. Niall's family were interviewed by the *Belfast Telegraph* and tried to drum up some support for the band. Bobby said, 'I am so proud of him. I would love to see him win it. I think Irish votes could be the difference between One Direction winning and not winning the show – it could hang on getting [voted-out Irish singer] Mary Byrne's Irish voters on board.'

Maura chipped in, too, saying, 'It would be the biggest dream ever for Niall to win *The X Factor*. They are winners for even getting into the final, but I know in their little hearts that they will be disappointed if they don't.' Because Byrne had left the show at the semifinal, there was, as Maura, too, pointed out, a chance that any Irish voters who had been phoning in for Byrne would transfer their allegiances to Niall's band.

'Mary was on the radio the other day and she said she wants all her votes to transfer to Niall, which is absolutely lovely of her,' said Maura. 'Niall and the lads need everyone's votes. This is a huge thing for us and it's weird and he finds it the very same. They can't get over going out in a blacked-out car, and screaming girls and photographers everywhere.' Niall's brother Greg, too, spoke: 'I'm excited but nervous for him. He has inspired me but I'm too old for my dream to be a footballer. My dream now is to see him have his dream.'

Niall's friend Adam Keena also spoke to reporters, highlighting how Niall's success had made others in the town believe they could make something big of their lives. 'Not many people from a small town like Mullingar believe that they can actually become something but Niall has actually changed everyone's perspective on that,' he said. 'He has inspired us all to believe that we can make something of ourselves if we try hard enough.'

The town was full of excitement. The Greville Arms Hotel was busy arranging an *X Factor* party. The hotel's owner described the place as 'buzzing'. A local nightclub, the Bed, also put on a special bash. His principal at the Coláiste Mhuire CBS, Joe O'Meara, said in the *Herald*, 'He is such an exceptional lad. He has found his niche big time and he is on top of the world. He's a lovely, unassuming guy and very well mannered. When he got *The X Factor* he came in to ask me could he postpone his Leaving Cert and he is welcome back at any time. We'd love to have him back.'

As the week wore on, good-luck messages mounted from the show-business world for Niall's band. Members of the Wanted sent their best wishes, as did former *X Factor* winners including Alexandra Burke and Joe McElderry. As part of the pre-final week, finalists traditionally visit their home towns to galvanize support and provide diverting footage to be aired for the final. However, heavy snow meant that the band were unable to fly over Ireland to visit Mullingar. Niall was disappointed: he is so proud of where he comes from and wanted to show it to his bandmates. In place of the visit, One Direction did a live interview with Ireland FM radio station from Granada Studios, Manchester. 'It was brilliant fun.' said Niall, looking on the bright side.

He got to see his bandmates' hometowns, though. In Liam's Wolverhampton they performed in front of five thousand excited locals, with the police having to hold some of the more excited fans back. They also rolled into Doncaster, Louis' hometown, where hundreds of people cheered them on at the singer's old school. In Holmes Chapel, Cheshire, Harry proudly took in the scene as his neighbours waved banners with his and the band's names on them. Zayn was aghast when he saw the crowd that had gathered at his local music store in Bradford in Yorkshire. Though Niall was sad not to encounter similar emotions due to the enforced cancellation of the Ireland trip, he had gained excitement by proxy. And the fact that One Direction had visited four hometowns during the week gave extra colour to their VTs on the final live shows. The other finalists – Rebecca Ferguson, Matt Cardle and Cher Lloyd – had, of course, visited only one town each.

Many commentators assumed that it was a foregone conclusion that One Direction would win the series. After all, it was reasoned, there was no more committed army to have on your side than that of excited teenage girls. Furthermore, it was argued, One Direction had the all-important backing of the show's boss, Simon Cowell. However, keen students of reality-television history would argue that neither assumption was infallible. After all, in 2002's series *Popstars: The Rivals*, which pitched a boy band against a girl band, it was taken for granted that the boy band would go on to have the more successful career. However, few remember One True Voice, the male five-piece that imploded soon after the show's climax, while few have forgotten Girls Aloud, the all-conquering female band spawned by the show.

Cowell's patronage, meanwhile, is not as decisive as conspiracy theorists may believe. Such a committed workhorse and focused figure is Cowell that he would never risk derailing a show in order to twist his act to the top spot.

Above: Isn't he cute? Niall as a baby on his 18th birthday cake.
Below: Niall with his parents, Maura and Bobby, and his brother Greg.

Left: From solo singer…

Below: … to boy band: One Direction is born.

Above: Getting used to the limelight: posing with mentor Simon Cowell.

Right: *X Factor* finalist Niall arrives at the studio with Nicky Byrne from Westlife.

Above: The boys quickly attract adoring fans wherever they go.
Below: Messing about – but the fans know who's who.

Left: Ready to rock after meeting fans outside *The X Factor* studios.

Below: Following in the footsteps of the Beatles.

Above: On the red carpet at the Pride of Britain Awards.
Below: With fellow *X Factor* contestants, including eventual winner Matt Cardle, at the world premiere of *Harry Potter and the Deathly Hallows: Part 1.*

Above: The teen heartthrobs pose with signed copies of their book *Dare to Dream*.

Below: Having the time of their lives: celebrating as their debut single 'What Makes You Beautiful' tops the UK charts.

Niall at the signing of the 1D debut album, *Up All Night* – the fastest-selling album of 2011.

The final would be split over two evenings, with an act eliminated on Saturday and Sunday, and a final two would battle it out as the climax to Sunday's show. Niall received a rude awakening on Saturday morning when a poll published in the *Sun* placed One Direction in third place, ahead of Lloyd but behind Ferguson, with Cardle in top spot. This positioning certainly shook up the expectations of some – and it proved prescient. Niall did his best to put the survey, which was splashed across the front page of the tabloid, out of his mind as he and the band went through their last-ditch rehearsals. As a keen football fan, Niall might have almost felt as if he were part of a team entering the FA Cup final. He dearly hoped that he would be celebrating as the winner by the end of the weekend.

Their first number was the Elton John track 'Your Song'. Walsh was as impressed as ever, and he would single out Niall in his feedback. 'Hey, One Direction, you're in the final – I hope you're here tomorrow night,' he said. 'It's amazing how five guys have gelled so well. I know you're all best friends. I've never seen a band cause so much hysteria so early in their career. I definitely think that you've got an amazing future. Niall, everybody in Ireland must vote for Niall, yes!'

Minogue echoed Walsh's wish. 'Guys, you have worked so hard in this competition. You were thrown together.

You deserve to be here and I'd love to see you in the final tomorrow.'

Cowell said that the first two performances by Cardle and Ferguson were 'so good' that his 'heart was sinking' over his band's potential on the night. However, he said, the band 'gave it one thousand per cent' and added, 'It's been an absolute pleasure working with you'. Lest his contribution sound like a send-off, bookmarking the band's *X Factor* experience, he added, 'I really hope people bother to pick up the phone, put you through to tomorrow, because you deserve to be there.'

The highlight of the performances for Niall came when they sang with Robbie Williams. They had performed in front of the legend during rehearsals, and he offered them plenty of encouragement. Once the cameras were rolling, Niall could scarcely believe he was about to sing on stage with the Take That and solo superstar. Williams entered the stage to join them in their rendition of his hit 'She's the One', with typical charisma. During the song's highest note, Williams turned to face the band and then high-fived each in turn in recognition of the fact they had all reached it. None of the band were able to contain their excitement. Each looked thrilled and disbelieving of the experience. Even Zayn smiled, for goodness' sake!

At the end of the song, Robbie shouted, 'The lads –

One Direction! Phone in!' And then he and the five band members disappeared into a group hug. Robbie then lifted Niall into the air. Touchingly, Niall recalls in *Dare to Dream* that as he was being lifted, the main thing on his mind was to hope someone had caught the moment on camera.

Speaking for the band on the night, Louis described himself as 'an absolutely massive Robbie fan. Thank you so much for doing this with us.' Williams nonchalantly replied, 'Oh, it's a pleasure – you guys rock!'

Summing up the mood, Cowell described Williams as 'a great friend to the show – very, very generous with his time – and he's made these boys' night of their lives.' For many viewers, the sheer enthusiasm of Niall and his band during the song with Williams was enough to mark it out as the highlight of the various finalists' duets. Cardle had sung with Rihanna, Ferguson had duetted with Christina Aguilera, and Cher Lloyd had performed with Black Eyed Peas star Will.i.am. The excitement with which One Direction had greeted their time on stage with Robbie had helped to send Niall's band through the first public vote of the weekend. It had been a particularly tense wait as O'Leary drew out the results announcement. At that stage, it was Cher Lloyd who was sent home, leaving One Direction to scrap it out with Cardle and Ferguson on the Sunday evening. Thus far, the poll in the *Sun*, then, was being proved correct.

Niall did his best to get some sleep on Saturday evening as he anticipated what was ahead and how far he had come. As he had queued up in Dublin to audition as a solo star, little could he have believed he would make it all the way to the final, knocking out thousands of other hopefuls. He could scarcely have predicted, either, that he would be in the final as part of a band, alongside four young English lads he had never met prior to the show.

In the final the following evening, each of the three remaining finalists would sing a song, before another act was eliminated. One Direction chose 'Torn', the Natalie Imbruglia track they had sung at the judges'-houses phase. It was a shrewd choice: the performance reminded viewers of the band's debut appearance together and showed their development since. Viewers recalled the sense that One Direction was *their* band, who had been formed in front of their eyes.

The emotion and tension in the air was palpable, as the band lined up to hear the judges' response. Walsh told them, 'You've got brilliant chemistry. I love the harmonies. I love the song choice. And we've got five new pop stars!'

A smiling Minogue added, 'Guys, you've done all the right things to make your place here in the final. That was a fantastic performance. Whatever happens tonight, I'm sure you guys are going to go on and release records and be the next big band.'

When Cole spoke, she again struck a tone that sounded as if she were calling time on the band's place in the contest. 'It's been so lovely to watch you guys from your first audition. To think that was only a few months ago! I really believe that you've got a massive future ahead of you and I wanna say thank you for being such lovely guys to be around.'

It was left to their mentor Cowell to speak in terms of the band's reaching the very climax of the evening. 'Let's be clear: anyone who comes into this final has got a great chance of bettering their future,' he said. 'But this is a competition and, in terms of the competition, in terms of who's worked the hardest, who I think deserves to win based on the future of something we haven't seen before, I would love to hear your names read out at the end of the competition – because I think you deserve it.'

Then, it was time for the results. The voting lines were frozen and O'Leary, describing the evening as 'very tense', announced that he had the results of the public vote. Louis, wearing a hooded jumper over a white T-shirt, exhaled anxiously as he waited. This time, the presenter announced who was through, rather than who was leaving. Before announcing the first name, he embarked on the customary, agonizing pause. As the acts waited, Niall lifted his hands in a, perhaps unconscious, gesture of prayer. After Cardle's name was called, Niall turned round to Cowell, as if in search of a hint of whether it would be his act or Ferguson who would take the last remaining place. Having appeared to have sought guidance from God, he was now seeking guidance from a man who some might say *believed* he was God. Cowell put a protective hand on Niall's shoulder.

When Ferguson's name was called, Niall looked to be one of the calmer members of the rejected band. He was the first to sportingly applaud Ferguson. He was showing the maturity and good manners that made his parents so proud. He managed a few wistful smiles as he watched the 'best bits' video that the show immediately aired. Louis, perhaps appropriately as he is the band's eldest member, was the first to speak following this crushing blow. 'It's been absolutely incredible,' he said. 'For me, the highlight was when we first sang together at the judges' houses. That was unbelievable. And you know what? We've done our absolute best, we've worked hard.'

Zayn, looking to the future, added a defiant note. 'We're definitely going to stay together. This isn't the last of One Direction!'

Cowell said 'Do you know what? I'm absolutely gutted for them.' He thanked those who had 'bothered to pick up the phone' and vote for the band, and added, 'This is just the beginning for these boys.'

As O'Leary dubbed the band 'absolute troopers', it was time for them to leave the stage. Niall managed a taut nod as they left.

As the show carried on without them, One Direction could only sit backstage and watch. Suddenly, Niall was, officially speaking, an outsider. Matt Cardle was eventually announced as the winner of the series. Within minutes of being crowned he was singing his winner's single, 'When We Collide'. As the song reached its final third, the other finalists stormed the stage to celebrate with him, as per *X Factor* tradition. The first to embrace the winner was, suitably enough, Niall. His warm and friendly nature could not be overshadowed by his disappointment. Niall then moved to the front of the stage to whip the audience into increasingly noisy cheering.

From start to finish of his *X Factor* journey, Niall Horan had remained as grounded as one could hope. There were no tantrums or sulks from him as his band finished in third place. Instead, as the curtains came down on the series, he was enjoying the moment and trying to heighten the excitement for the freshly crowned champion. Gestures such as this stand out at such landmark television moments. His band may have finished third, but Niall's big heart was already winning over the nation.

CHAPTER FOUR

X + 1D = SUCCESS

After the series climax, came the confounding comedown.

As Niall and the band packed their things and moved out of *The X Factor* house the morning after the final, they had mixed feelings. They were obviously disappointed to have finished third, but they already sensed that they would not be returning to the lives they had led before they entered *The X Factor* world. They did not, for instance, return to their homes, but instead were checked into a west London hotel. They rolled up to *The X Factor* series 'wrap' party, suited and booted. Niall wore a blue blazer with a light-grey shirt and dark-grey trousers, looking very smart for the cameras. Yet inside he was feeling anxious about what the immediate future would bring. His state of mind now was less that of a roller coaster and more that of a vehicle not quite knowing which way it would turn next.

At this point the band were indeed at a crossroads themselves: they would either get a record deal and continue the exciting, celebrity lifestyle of recent months, or they would experience that soul-destroying comedown that a lot of *X Factor* finalists face after each series ends. For those in the latter camp it can be tough to readjust to normal life. For a short while, rejected finalists enjoy a fame of sorts. Social-network websites such as Twitter continue to buzz about them for a while, and they may get minor mentions in the mainstream press for a time, or even invitations to some glittering gatherings. However, as the fuss dies down, the acts can feel crushed. Having been handed a brief glimpse of life as a pop star only for such stature to be denied them, some acts wonder if they would prefer not to have had that glittering life in their sights in the first place. Fame can be a cruel drug, particularly if it appears and disappears with great haste. Niall did not want to go the way of his sometime live bill partner Lloyd Daniels.

Fortunately, Cowell was determined that the band be snapped up. Niall would not be surrendering his fame any time soon. Cowell called the band to a private meeting. Although the show was over, for Niall, when he and the band sat down with Cowell, it felt in a sense as if he was back on air. This was because Cowell could not resist the temptation to ham it up with a few *X Factor*-style dramatic pauses. In *Dare to Dream*, Cowell recalls saying, 'I've made a decision', before letting the tension hang for a while. As Niall later reflected, the guru can rarely resist taking people down to build them up – or vice versa. Eventually, after waiting so long that the boys could hardly breathe, he told them that he had, indeed, decided to sign them. Niall and the others exploded with joy. Harry even burst into tears. A proud and expectant Cowell told his new band, 'You have to enjoy yourselves. You're going to make a lot of money, but you have to enjoy every single minute of it.'

In an interview with *Rolling Stone*, Cowell has since opened the lid on the behind-the-scenes machinations that led up this meeting. He had invited rival divisions within the Sony Corporation to make pitches to him before he decided which label the band would sign with. Normally, the possessive Cowell would insist they come to his Syco division. He was so aware of the band's potential, though, that he wanted to consider other options. 'This was such an important signing, we let three or four of the Sony labels make a presentation,' he said. 'I didn't automatically give it to my own label. I thought, "This is so important, if somebody can come up with a better idea . . ." I was actually willing to pass them along to another division of Sony because I thought the group were that important.' For a control freak such as Cowell, these words were revealing. If anyone wanted an upfront indication that something big might be on the cards, there was one right there.

The band members then went their separate ways to spend Christmas with their families and friends. But such moments of domestic tranquillity were about to become a rarity for Niall. With One Direction's seasonal break over, Niall flew back to London to be reunited with the others. Their debut task as a band was one to be envied. As their families and friends back in Ireland and the UK battled with the cold winter, Niall and his band jetted to Los Angeles. On arrival in Tinseltown, he was delighted to discover that the sun was shining and the city itself was glittering with a galaxy of stars. The visit was a combination of work – including a recording session in a studio and a meeting with top music producer Max Martin and *American Idol* guru Randy Jackson – and also some leisure time, including sightseeing and shopping. They also shopped at the famous outdoor mall The Grove, where they met up with fellow finalist Cher Lloyd. The band stayed at the luxurious W hotel, which sits majestically in Beverly Hills. The huge rooms the boys stayed in stunned them. The eyes of Niall, a boy from small-town, Ireland, spread wide indeed during the stay.

However, it was when they arrived back in Britain that the band got their most dramatic glimpse of the life ahead of them, the shape of their most frenzied encounter with their fans to date. Niall and the band were confronted with hundreds of screaming fans when they arrived at Heathrow Airport. Security staff had to grab the boys and escort them at great speed to a police van, to avoid their being crushed by the fans. Some of the band really enjoyed the experience. Louis, for example, 'got a real buzz' from it, but Niall was terrified and freaked out. He is the band member who has found it hardest to adjust to such encounters.

As an amusing aside, it's worth recording that former Boyzone lead singer Ronan Keating, a heartthrob back in the 1990s, was also arriving around the same time. Once upon a time he was mobbed by fans; now he was an onlooker as girls ran screaming at other pop stars, including fellow countryman Niall. Keating wrote on Twitter, 'Just landed at Heathrow and when I walked out there were hundreds of screaming Fans Sadly not for me HaHa. One direction were on flight. X' Still, the experience will have brought back fond memories for Keating: the Irish security specialist who was subsequently hired to look after the band had worked with Boyzone at their peak, as well as other top pop acts, including Westlife and Girls Aloud.

The hysterical female reaction was one of the most striking parts of fame that Niall had to adjust to quickly. Another, tangentially related, aspect of celebrity life was the way he would from now on be linked with a bevy of beauties in the pages of tabloid newspapers and celebrity magazines. During *The X Factor*, it was suggested he was dating various members of the contest's girl band Belle Amie, including Rebecca Creighton and Sophia Wardman. Then, *Buzz* magazine suggested he had been trying his luck with Cheryl Cole. Had these rumours been accurate, Niall would have been a very busy and excitable young man. While the speculation took a bit of getting used to for Niall, he would soon learn to take it in his stride, particularly when Harry became the centre of such tabloid obsession that he took the heat for the other four members of the band.

On their return, they moved in together into a London complex. He told *The Late, Late Show* that the move to London was working well. 'We all live in the same complex, we go to work, come back, sleep, eat,' he said. But they did not settle in one city for long: soon it was time for more screams and hysteria for One Direction as they joined *The X Factor Live* tour. The preparations kicked off in February 2011, at the Light Structures venue in Birmingham. Here, the stage presence and confidence they had built up during *The X Factor* live shows was honed and refined by a series of expert coaches. The rehearsals and the drilling were serious: they went over some parts of their slot more than twenty times. It was hard work but it would all pay off during the thirty-seven-date live tour, which turned into an unforgettable experience for all five members of the band.

Niall will never forget the opening night in Birmingham. Some twelve thousand *X Factor* fans squeezed into the venue to see the band and the other finalists. Never before had a third-placed act received such loud cheers as One Direction did. It was almost as if they were the headline act. Accordingly, then, in a break with convention they were allowed to sing five songs – the same number as the series winner. All the other acts, including the second-placed Rebecca Ferguson, were given only two songs to sing. At last, the suspicions of other *X Factor* artists that One Direction were being favoured seemed to have some truth to them.

However, the decision to give them extra songs was vindicated, as far as the tour organizers were concerned at least, by the deafening din that greeted the band when they took to the stage. As they appeared in lifts from under the stage. They sang 'Kids in America' and 'Only Girl (in the World)', two of the most uplifting and anthemic tracks they had sung during *The X Factor* live shows. The evidence of their latest dance lessons was clear as they owned the stage as they never previously had.

Then came a twist: they were not only allowed to perform, but they also sang a song that they had not performed on television. It was, in fact, a song they would only have sung had they reached the final two: 'Forever Young', what would have been their winner's single. Then they sang two more live-show songs: 'Chasing Cars' and 'My Life Would Suck Without You'. The screams with which their every track and between-songs utterances were greeted was phenomenal. Their fellow acts would have been forgiven for feeling a pang of envy.

However, any envy was mostly put aside during some fun-packed nights. On the tour, they shared a dressing room with the other male finalists. This meant that they were reunited with Matt Cardle as well as two artists who had been eliminated earlier in the competition, Aiden Grimshaw and the clownish Wagner. Such fun. Cardle had originally declined the offer to have, as the series winner, a dressing room of his own. However, within a few nights of One Direction's craziness he decided that he would take the solo dressing room after all.

After each show they would head to the respective city's hotel, where they would party into the early hours. On two separate occasions they ended up having memorable 'fruit fights'. The first, in Sheffield, lasted for five fantastic minutes. It all kicked off when Louis casually tried to launch an apple core into the bin. There was a 'second-leg' fruit fight in Liverpool. Other fun and frolics on tour included contests to incorporate random words or phrases into their onstage banter. These included 'winklepickers' and 'shower cubicle'. It all helped the tour pass quickly.

Niall's favourite city on the tour was Dublin – not, he insists, just because he grew up near there. 'The crowd were just incredible,' he wrote in *Dare to Dream*. 'It was so loud and when we came out of the arena I felt like I'd been on a plane for seven hours – my ears were popping.' They did five shows in the Irish capital and Niall felt that each one was louder than its predecessor.

The Horan family attended one of the shows, and he was thrilled that they were handed prime seats. They came to relax with him in the hotel after the show. Then it was off to Belfast, where, Niall felt, there was also a special buzz in the air. 'I couldn't believe how much support we had.' He had a chuckle at some of the banners the fans had brought, and chatted with as many as he could outside the venues and back at the hotels they stayed in.

A few weeks after the tour, Niall found himself in the midst of an eerie but amusing coincidence, as described in

Dare to Dream. He, Liam and Zayn popped into a Tesco branch and, as they were queuing up to pay, they noted that the chap in front of them in the queue wore a hat similar to that of series champion Matt Cardle. When the man in question turned round, they discovered that it *was* Cardle. 'What are the chances of that happening?' asked Niall.

At this stage, the band were in a slightly strange position. They had yet to release any material of their own, yet they were one of the most talked-about bands in the country. Not only that but they had already published their first official book, *Forever Young*, and signed an endorsement deal with Nintendo for their DS Pokémon game. The advert for the latter deal saw them mucking about in a hotel room while playing the game. For this, and for lending their names to the project, they were paid handsomely. In the wake of the deal, Niall became so obsessed with the game that he began to play it even while sitting on the toilet. (You could be forgiven for wondering at this stage whether Niall spent more time on the toilet than most. The truth is that his time in the smallest room just seems to be more eventful than that of most people.)

The band embarked on a signing tour to drum up sales of *Forever Young*, and Niall loved the chance to meet even more of their growing and devoted fan base. The crowds who arrived were so plentiful and loud that Niall would end the sessions with a headache. 'There wasn't a single moment where it went quiet,' he wrote in the book's follow-up book, *Dare to Dream*. 'The support the fans showed us was brilliant. I got given seven pairs of large plastic Shamrock glasses.' One can never have enough of those.

Then, it was time for him and the band to continue work on what would be their debut album. They were so excited they hugged each other. They recorded it in several countries, including Stockholm, the USA and the UK. No wonder the band described it as a 'really intense' experience. For their debut single they had sky-high standards. They wanted it to be amazing for two reasons: first, they wanted to reward and delight the fan base that had already built around them before they had released anything; second, they wanted to confound the cynics. The band were only too aware that many commentators and ordinary members of the public saw them as pop puppets. Scepticism over Simon Cowell, *The X Factor* and his entire pop empire seemed to grow by the year. With the band having been formed on the show and then mentored by Cowell himself, they had a lot to work against in the eyes of some. Therefore, they were as disinclined to accept a forgettable factory-line pop tune as they were to release a tried-and-tested cover. They wanted something special which would blow everyone, fans and cynics alike, away.

To this end, they worked with a top-notch team of producers and songwriters on their material, from which the single would eventually be chosen. An early word on what was coming together came from one of the team, Savan Kotecha, the songwriter who had composed tracks for the likes of Britney Spears, JLS and Leona Lewis. He told the band's early online champion, the entertainment-news magazine *Digital Spy*, 'For them it's just going to be experimenting with a few things – they're going to be fine. They've got some really good songs. The stuff I've heard has been really catchy and everyone loves the guys, so it's just about capturing that in the music, which I think is what they're going to be doing.'

The track that was eventually chosen as their debut single was 'What Makes You Beautiful'. It opens with a staccato guitar riff. It is up-tempo, with an impish flavour. It sounds almost as if it could be heralding a McFly song. Immediately, Niall's band were showing that they were not setting out just to sing dreamy, string-sodden boy-band anthems. There would be no sitting on, then rising from, stools here. Then the cymbal ushers in the first verse. Liam, in deep, semi-raunchy tones with an accent tinged with American, addresses the subject of the song: a girl who does not know she is beautiful. The track is enriched as it hits the first bridge, which is sung by Harry.

Then Niall and the rest of the band join in for its explosive and addictive chorus. Even before the infectious 'You don't know-oh-oh' first rings out, you're hooked. Zayn and Harry take care of the second verse, with Niall having to content himself with joining in on the choruses and the 'na na-na na' chant that precedes the middle eight. The longer the song goes on the more catchy it becomes. So lively is it that it would be a musical crime if it ended with a gradual fade – and it doesn't. Instead, a final vocal blast of 'That's what makes you beautiful', courtesy of Harry, closes the three minutes and eighteen seconds of pop fun. Written by Rami Yacoub, Carl Falk and Savan Kotecha, it was majestic. It was as compelling a pop debut as anyone in the industry could remember. Its debut airplay was on Scott Mills's Radio 1 show on 10 August. Niall joined the rest of the band in a celebratory dance and huddle as the song was first shared with the outside world. Fans across the country bordered on meltdown.

That meltdown was matched by preorders: three weeks before the song was released it was announced that it had attracted the highest ever number of pre-orders for a Sony act. The reactions of media critics only fuelled the frenzy of excitement. *Digital Spy*'s Robert Copsey said the subject of the song was 'That endangered breed who are visually stunning but aren't aware of it'. He gave it four out of five stars, and described it as a cross between Pink and McFly. He concluded, 'Like a Forever Friends bear from your high school crush, it's adorable, completely innocent and bound to cause a stir amongst your mates.'

A less likely champion was *NME*. Ailbhe Malone declared it as 'so unthreatening it might have to think twice about holding hands, lest it get overwhelmed'. However, she said this was not 'a bad thing'. The fact that these critics liked the song was pleasing, but for Niall the fact that they 'got' what it was about was just as gratifying. He has always seen music as much as a tool of communication as one of mere entertainment.

Taking the sort of 'muso' view of the song that Niall would have enjoyed, Malone continued with an unsurprisingly technical musical look at the song: 'Channelling their sterling performance of "My Life Would Suck Without You", "What Makes You Beautiful" is exuberant with a catchy "oh na na na" middle eight. The real genius is that the chord progression is simple enough to be played on an acoustic guitar at a house party.' *PopMatters* loved it too: 'it is a nice get-up-and-go dance number (complete with cowbell!)'. The CBBC *Newsround* website gave the single four stars out of five, saying, 'Think summer, think sunshine, think parties on the beach with your mates, and you'll get the general vibe of "What Makes You Beautiful". It's classic pop – fun, upbeat and incredibly catchy.' It was indeed catchy – for a while it seemed as if everywhere you went someone was signing or whistling the 'you don't know-oh-oh' of the chorus. Niall was thrilled to be providing the soundtrack to a nation.

The single's promotional video, which rarely seemed to leave the airwaves for long, was filmed on a California beach. Niall found it hard to believe his luck as they shot the scenes in such blissful surroundings, with attractive female 'extras' involved in the shoot. Although the band reportedly worked eighteen hours on the first day of the shoot and fourteen hours on the second day, Niall kept his feet on the ground and realized that being filmed on a luxurious American beach was not an experience to complain about. During a break in the filming they also recorded a video of themselves singing the Oasis track 'Wonderwall'. Niall provided the musical backing on his acoustic guitar. The video would be released on YouTube in the coming months, another reminder that the band members are fans of more adult, rock-based material than their releases would indicate.

With the critics and fans onside, and record-breaking preorders already under their belts, Niall and his bandmates dared to dream that they might be sitting on a number-one hit. They counted the days until it was released with growing anticipation. 'I'm excited because it's what I've been working towards all my life and it's finally happening,' said Zayn in an interview with *Top of the Pops* magazine. He spoke for all of the band. It was released on 11 September 2011. That day, the band were flown by private helicopter across the country to greet fans who had queued to see them. In the chopper were plush leather seats, computer games to play and plenty of treats to snack on. It was a whirlwind day of promotional appearances and interviews, including with the Dublin radio station 98FM, a particularly enjoyable slot for Niall.

On the Sunday after the release, the band gathered at Radio 1 studios to hear the chart rundown. Given the level of preorders and the growing frenzy around the band, it was not the biggest shock in pop history when it was announced that 'What Makes You Beautiful' was the week's No. 1, displacing Pixie Lott. All the same, this was a moment of huge significance. Niall and the others cheered loudly when the news was announced.

The thousand-plus-strong crowd of fans outside screamed their own joy. The single had racked up the highest first-week sales of any UK single released that year. This fact blew Niall's mind at the time – but breaking records would quickly become a fact of life for One Direction. The band celebrated with their mentor Simon Cowell, who took them to a posh fundraising dinner at the Savoy hotel in London. The boys looked decidedly dapper in their black suits and ties. Leona Lewis, Cowell's other prized act, joined them. There was an auction to raise funds for the Katie Piper Foundation, a charity of which Cowell is a patron. During the auction, Niall inadvertently made a 'bid'. Harry, ever the prankster, stole Niall's bidding card and placed an £8,000 bid on an item without his knowing. Fortunately, Niall avoided a big bill when someone else placed a higher bid. As for Liam, he was just thrilled that his long-term crush Leona Lewis was there.

Now that he'd enjoyed a big milestone in his career, it was time for Niall to celebrate a major milestone in his life: his eighteenth birthday. As Liam had celebrated his own birthday a few weeks before, the band decided to have, effectively, a joint bash. Wearing a dark-blue coat with light-blue trousers and green trainers, Niall looked at the casual end of the smart–casual spectrum. They kicked off proceedings in the bar of the Sanderson Hotel before moving on to the clubs, Movida and Chinatown. The band had earlier presented Niall with a novel present: a waxwork of President Barack Obama. Liam explained why they chose such a gift. 'Niall is obsessed with Barack Obama,' he told the *Sun*. 'He knows everything about him. We looked around for the waxwork for ages. It's a life-size model and it's heavy. We had it made and delivered. We all chipped in for it. He sits on a bench in our flat. Niall loves it. It was a fair bit of money but I can't say, as we don't want Niall to know.' Whatever the price, Niall was chuffed to bits. 'It's such a good present. I love Obama,' he said. 'Who knows, maybe next year I'll get Michelle, too.'

On and on the partying went. During a performance at London's G-A-Y nightclub the band continued the Niall-focused festivity, presenting him with a giant birthday cake on stage. Naturally, a food fight soon broke out and Niall was, as it were, caked with cake, as were his bandmates. The stage, too, became a mess and, when the band subsequently sang 'What Makes You Beautiful', Harry slipped over. Niall, the birthday boy, managed to keep his footing. He showed how, figuratively speaking, one can have one's cake and eat it. It had been just the sort of eighteenth birthday most teenage boys would dream of: night after night of riotous fun with your mates, finishing up with a food fight. Although much of it was played out under the public glare, it was still, at its heart, a down-to-earth time. The boy from Ireland was a whole lot wiser, but he had not changed in any negative way.

*

Then, it was time for the debut album to be unleashed upon the expectant British teenage population. 'We're pretty proud of it,' said Niall at the time on entertainment news magazine *Digital Spy*. Called *Up All Night*, it emerged as a shrewdly compiled, fizzingly produced piece of work. After its upbeat opener, 'What Makes You Beautiful', the first change in tempo and genre comes right away: in contrast to the opener, the second track, 'It's Gotta Be You', is a true boy-band ballad. Just the sort of song Dannii Minogue wanted the band to sing on *The X Factor*. Here, the lyric is full of regret for pain that has been unintentionally caused to a girl. Every listener can relate to the expressed wish that time could be rewound. The chorus tells the girl that there is no one but her. Lush strings turn this into a cinematic song that delights the listener. No wonder it was chosen as a subsequent single!

The third song is 'One Thing', almost an echo, musically, of 'What Makes You Beautiful'. It includes the memorable line 'Shot me out of the sky – you're my Kryptonite'. It is a song of much fun, cheek and energy. It is one of Niall's two favourite songs on the album. 'More Than This', however, is the slowest and gentlest track on the album. The lyric, about dying inside when the narrator sees the girl lie down with another guy, hits the listener hard. The track features some astonishing falsetto vocals, which show the range of the band and add true gravitas to the experience. The album's title tune, 'Up All Night', is the fifth track. Set to a guitar track reminiscent of McFly or even their pop predecessors Busted, it is an account of a raucous teenage party, with its shaking floor, people 'going all the way', broken tables, Katy Perry on the sound system. It is a hedonist's call to arms to a party generation. This is Niall's other personal favourite.

'I Wish' is a mid-tempo sound very much in the album-track mode, while 'Tell Me a Lie' is a song that oozes America. Here they had an eye on the States. Its successor, 'Taken', is, in contrast, a tune that can to be sung around a bonfire anywhere, complete with acoustic guitars so beloved of Niall. If the next song, 'I Want', reminded listeners of a mid-career track by McFly, that is for good reason: their chief songwriter Tom Fletcher wrote it. Fletcher made some catty remarks about One Direction when they first emerged into the pop scene, but he quickly realized they could be a cash cow for his songs. Niall, who had enjoyed Fletcher's handiwork since he was a little kid watching Busted sing Fletcher-written tracks, was delighted. 'Everything About You' was one of the first tracks the band recorded. 'Straight off the show, into the studio,' said Niall on Twitter about the laying down of the track. 'Same Mistakes' is a sugary, rolling ballad. The rich backing track gently enhances the vocals of Niall and company. In the penultimate track, the band say they want to save a girl from her current lot in life.

And so 'Save You Tonight' – musically a song that could easily be performed by JLS or the Wanted – pushes all the right buttons. For a moment, when the final track kicks in, the listener's ear is tricked into wondering if it is a cover of Taio Cruz's 'Dynamite'. Then, during the bridge, the song momentarily reminds one of Rihanna's 'Only Girl (in the World)'. An impressive anthem ends an impressive album.

Niall's parts on the album were slightly limited. His line 'now I'm climbing the walls' was probably the best known of his vocal solos. However, another standout one comes in 'More Than This', when his delivery of the verse beginning 'I'm louder, would you see me?' is a powerful and emotional highlight of the track. He sings the lines plaintively, every bit living up to the meaning of lyric. Then there is his playful solo in 'One Thing', for part of which he is joined by a harmonizing Zayn.

He also has briefer, less consequential, solos in other tracks, including 'Save You Tonight'. In the future, Niall would have fuller parts in the band's music, as his stature grew. However, he could be proud of his part in *Up All Night*, an album that was constructed in the days when Liam and, particularly, Harry, were still seen as the standout members. So much would change in that regard.

Working on the album, the band had hooked up with a string of impressive names. Wayne Hector had written for

Westlife, Steve Robson had worked with James Morrison and Busted. Perhaps the two people they worked with who most excited the boys were Red One, who has co-produced a string of hits for Lady Gaga, and Ed Sheeran, the singer-songwriter sensation. The Sheeran link-up was one that particularly excited Niall. As a regular toter of an acoustic guitar himself, Niall was thrilled to work with the ginger-haired genius. 'Getting to write and record with Ed Sheeran on our album was an honour,' he gushed in the *Daily Star*. Fleshing out what the singer-songwriter meant to him away from the studio, he added: 'We're quite good friends with Ed. We always hang out with him. If you listen to Ed's album, you'll know that he is one of the best lyricists I've ever heard in my life. He knows how to string words together like you wouldn't imagine. We were very lucky to work with him.'

Harry shared Niall's excitement at it all, commenting that the people they worked with on the album were 'legendary'. What a team it was: there were twenty-two songwriters involved in the tracks on *Up All Night*. On top of this, the band members themselves get co-writing credits on three of the tracks. Niall had his first songwriting credits and he was yet to reach his twenties – not bad at all.

The album met with the approval of many critics. The *Sun*'s face of showbiz Gordon Smart declared, '*Up All Night* will be lapped up by their young fan-base' and praised it for its blend of sounds and styles. *Cosmopolitan* magazine felt that the album was full of 'toe-tappers that are just impossible to dislike'. The *Independent* said the album would 'sell by the zillion', while the *Daily Star* said it was full of 'belting fun pop anthems'. The album debuted at No. 2 in the UK charts. Impressive in itself – and things got more impressive still when it became the fastest-selling debut album on the UK Albums Chart of 2011. It also reached the Top 10 in other countries, including Sweden, Ireland, the Netherlands, New Zealand and Australia. We will turn to its US performance in the next chapter.

To tie in with the album's release, ITV2 broadcast a documentary entitled *One Direction: A Year in the Making*. This behind-the-scenes special lifted the lid on the first twelve months of the band. They had also by this stage appeared on the ITV show *Red or Black*, where they sang 'What Makes You Beautiful'. Harry struggled a bit with his vocals in the a capella section, prompting a tirade of vile remarks about him on the unforgiving public forum that is Twitter. Harry later logged onto the site and was shaken by what he saw. Niall sympathized. 'The stuff that people were saying about him was just disgusting,' said Niall on the documentary, with protective anger in his voice. 'No one wants to go and read that stuff about themselves, no matter who they are.' Not for the first time, and certainly not the last, Niall was the band member who was most naturally supportive of a colleague in trouble. Behind the scenes, he had quite a leadership role.

In the wake of the album's release, One Direction took to the road on their first ever headline tour. Niall was so excited as they set off – this was just what he had been dreaming of for so long. Beginning in the middle of December in Watford, they performed in cities across the UK and Ireland to fans who had snapped up every ticket on offer within minutes of their going on sale. They were fine shows. As well as singing familiar tracks from their album and its B-side 'Na, Na, Na', they also performed some cover versions. Among these were 'I Gotta Feeling', by the Black Eyed Peas, the Zutons/ Amy Winehouse track 'Valerie' and 'Use Somebody' by Kings of Leon. There were also 'snowball' fights with the plastic snowballs that were sent down from on high during one point in the set, followed later on by silver streamers.

With Niall plucking at his acoustic guitar for parts of the set and the band indulging in ample between-songs banter, the shows made for superb nights out. Naturally, the other ingredient of the experience was the screams of the fans who had been lucky enough to get tickets. Even seasoned concertgoers and staff at the venues were taken aback by

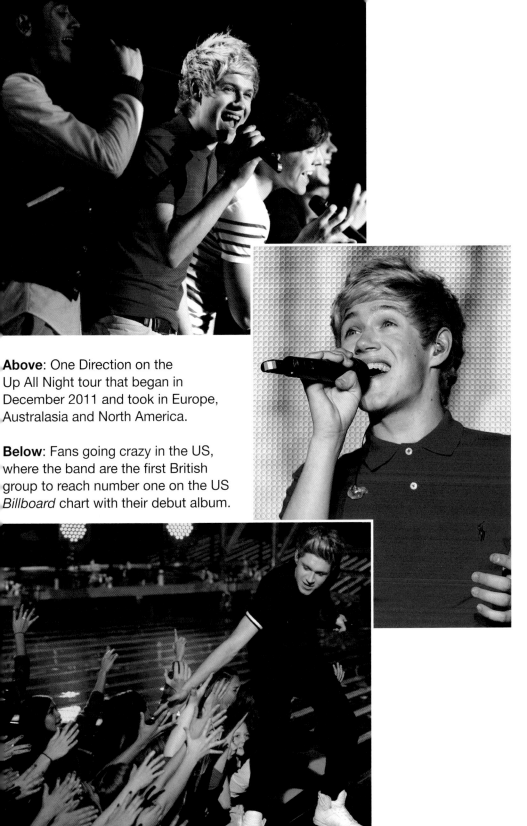

Above: One Direction on the Up All Night tour that began in December 2011 and took in Europe, Australasia and North America.

Below: Fans going crazy in the US, where the band are the first British group to reach number one on the US *Billboard* chart with their debut album.

Above: Looking smart at the BRIT Awards in 2012 where 1D won Best British Single for 'What Makes You Beautiful'.
Below: At the MTV Video Music Awards where 'What Makes You Beautiful' won Best Pop Video.

Above: At the *Men in Black 3* film premiere, New York.
Below: Speaking of men in black … looking smart again at the *GQ* Awards in London.

From talent-show contestants to global stars.

Left and above: Chilling out: Niall enjoying a well-deserved break in the US.

Below: At a football match with former girlfriend Amy Green.

Above: You know you've made it when you're immortalized at Madame Tussauds (New York).

Left: And when you've got your own doll!

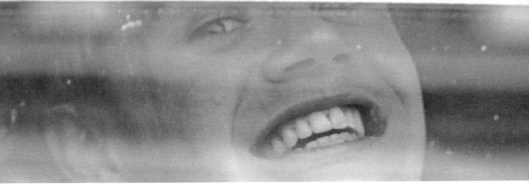

Above: Niall's all smiles – the braces are off!
Below: The boys win the BRIT Award for Global Success. One Direction have conquered the world and show no signs of stopping.

Niall looking dapper at his brother's wedding.

the volume of the noise. The only downside of the tour would come when their tour bus was smashed into by a car in early January 2012. Although three of the band, who were inside the bus at the time, got head and neck pains as well as shock, there were no serious injuries.

Towards the end of 2011 the lads attended *GQ* magazine's Men of the Year bash. This was a more grown-up gathering than many of the jollies they attended, with a guest list to match – a fact that thrilled Niall. 'Just being in the same room as Bono was great,' he told the magazine later. 'Stephen Fry's speech was incredible as well.' Though he felt fortunate to have his career and to be able to attend so many glittering teen bashes, Niall also wanted to roll up to more refined and adult gigs.

Another adult gathering came in the shape of the annual BRIT awards ceremony. Held at the O2 Arena in February for the second successive year, it was anchored by the band's friend, actor and comedian, James Corden. It turned out to be a bittersweet evening for One Direction. It all started so well: they were nominated in the Best British Single category. Given how many successful bands never win a BRIT during their career, it was quite an achievement that One Direction were already on the brink of winning their first. For their category, a public vote had been held to decide the winner, so the gong held extra clout. It was listeners to the Capital FM radio station who had voted, but, amid the excitement of winning the award, Harry accidentally thanked the listeners of Radio 1.

Louis had spoken first as they accepted the award. 'Wow,' he said, 'we cannot believe that we are stood here.' He then said that 'this award is for the fans'. Harry's fateful moment came next. After reprising Louis' thanks to the fans, he added, 'And a massive thank you to Radio 1.' The band's management sensed the gravity of the faux pas and quickly issued a statement through the band's official Twitter account. 'One Direction forgot to thank the Capital Radio listeners last night when picking up their Brit Award for "Best British Single", read the statement. 'This was an oversight as the boys were caught up in the excitement of winning. The band would like take this opportunity to thank Capital Radio and all their listeners for their support and for voting for them.' Niall, always one to unearth the positivity or humour in any situation, saw the funny side of it.

Meanwhile, though, the show had to go on and several members of the band seemingly got stuck into the complimentary refreshments. During a television interview later in the evening, Niall was flush-faced, while Harry slurred and mumbled. When they reappeared for an even later interview, Harry said nothing but merely pointed at the camera in a rather tired and emotional way. Later, they visited a McDonald's drive-thru, where Niall ordered a quarter-pounder with cheese, six chicken nuggets *and* a double cheeseburger. He had loved the evening from start to finish, including the opportunity it gave him to meet artists he admired, including the leader singer of the Script, Danny O'Donoghue. Niall also always enjoyed bumping into Katy Perry at such get-togethers. They share a sense of humour and enjoy looking back at the day she – only just – sent him through on *The X Factor*. She, in turn, is always thrilled to see him, and his bandmates, too. 'They've been so sweet to me every time I meet them,' she told the *Irish Sun*. 'I'm thrilled for the success they are enjoying and love hanging out with them – Niall is just lovely.'

In May 2012, as the band were busy preparing for an American tour scheduled for 2013, they visited a fan who was suffering with cancer. Niamh Power was thrilled to meet the boys, who were humbled by the experience. Niall later tweeted a photo accompanied by the message, 'Met this amazing girl this morning, Niamh! Great morning, brave girl.' The band have taken part in numerous charitable ventures, including visits to other sick children through the Rays of Sunshine charity; a Comic Relief dinner date in which the band pretended to be BA cabin crew; and the BBC Radio 1 Teen Awards, which recognize special teenagers. 'It's always good to be on a great bill,' Niall told BBC *Newsbeat*.

They had another hit with the Comic Relief single, for which they recorded a mash-up of 'One Way or Another (Teenage Kicks)'. They had visited Africa to see projects that would benefit from the single's sales. Perhaps their most iconic performance of the song came at the 2013 BRIT Awards. As well as picking up the Global Success prize at the ceremony in recognition of their worldwide record sales, they sang the Comic Relief mash-up. The success of the song stunned Niall. He said on RTÉ news: 'When the charity single went to No. 1 in sixty-two countries, I didn't even know sixty-two countries existed! We're definitely going to be performing in places I've never heard of before.'

All of these admirable ventures only swelled the popularity of One Direction. An arena tour, which Liam had foreshadowed at the BRITs shortly after Harry's slip-up, sold out in good time. The band duly did just that, unveiling a string of dates, beginning at London's O2 Arena on 22 February 2013. The fifteen dates sold out within a few minutes of going on sale. A list of twenty new shows was quickly added, including matinée performances in London, Cardiff, Manchester and Birmingham.

The speed with which they could sell out Britain's biggest arenas was awe-inducing: One Direction were, by this measure, the royalty of the UK pop scene. Their Irish

Prince Charming could hardly be more thrilled. Yet their pre-eminence was about to spread to other countries, including the most prized market of all. There, Niall would find that he would move from the margin of the band to, in the eyes of many, a central, starring role.

CHAPTER FIVE

STATESIDE AND DOWN UNDER

One Direction's jaw-dropping success in America has been widely discussed. Before recalling their exciting and conquering journey Stateside, it is worth stating at the offset that, for Niall, the One Direction American dream has extra resonance and significance. For it is at this stage in the story that his journey from the sidelines of the band to leading light reaches its fruition. For a variety of reasons, Niall transformed into a leading member who, at least, rivalled Harry Styles for the role of the band's most loved ingredient. According to a report in *Closer* magazine, it was

Niall who was taking the plaudits in America. 'All the boys are popular, but the girls in the US seem to be absolutely obsessed with Niall,' an insider told the magazine. 'They love the fact he's Irish and looks like the all-American boy. He gets swamped with girls wherever he goes.' The source continued, 'Zayn is a close second – he's very cheeky and confident, which is going down well. It's definitely been a knock to Harry's ego, as he's used to being the heartthrob back home. It's only natural that the boys are competing for attention. It's causing a bit of tension!'

Back home in England, members of the media were taking note of Niall's ascendancy in America. Soon, publications in the UK were pushing for Niall to take the crown in Britain, too. Perhaps, show-business reporters wondered, they had been too hasty in painting Harry as the unrivalled centrepiece of One Direction. *Metro* newspaper, for instance, headlined a story on Niall, 'Top 10 reasons Niall Horan is the most popular One Direction member: From his Irish charm to his single status'. Among the 10 reasons was one praising his wholesomeness: 'While Zayn's been in the press for allegedly cheating on his girlfriend, Perrie Edwards, Louis has lost his temper at 1D fans, Liam has admitted to having a wandering eye and Harry's had cougar after cougar in his bed, Niall can do no wrong.'

Other publications and online outlets followed suit,

including the ever-influential Sugarscape and *BOP/Tiger Beat*. The latter website included this among its 10 reasons: 'He's honest about who he is. It's like Niall just held up a sign to the world saying, "Hello world, this is me – this is what you get!" He's not ashamed of his love for food or his love for soccer. We love someone who is willing to geek out about what they love!'

Months later, the fans themselves spoke when they got the hashtag '#10ReasonILoveNiall' to trend on Twitter. One such tweet, from '@Jadore1Dx', read 'He's perfect, He's Irish, He sings, plays guitar, nicest accent, blue eyes, amazing laugh, cute, loves food & he's Niall.' Another Twitter Directioner, @AnisaPrihantini, wrote, 'Kind, cutes [sic], the one and only blond hair, youngest, sweets, famous, not handsome too, little Lazy, unique, dreamer . . '. Another typical comment came from the hand of @lexii_neumann, who wrote, 'He's beautiful. He can sing. He's Irish. His eyes. He's sweet. He's caring. His Smile. His laugh. His passion.' Sales of the band's official dolls also reflected Niall's rise. In 2011, for instance, Niall's dolls had been second-best-selling, shifting 17.9% of the total, compared with Harry's 35.5%. However, in 2012, Niall was top of the list. Of the official dolls sold, 25.2% were Niall dolls. Harry had moved into third place, with Louis in second.

*

Rumours of colossal tensions or resentments within the band – over which member is the most popular at any given time or in any given place – have been denied from within the camp. During the early days of One Direction, it was first rumoured that Liam considered himself a step ahead of the other boys owing to his previous *X Factor* experience and subsequent moderate regional progress as a solo singer. Then, it was said that Niall, Zayn and Louis resented both Liam and Harry for the central, starring roles they had carved themselves. Niall's brother Greg disputes all this. 'It's absolute nonsense,' he told the *Herald* in November 2012. 'The boys all get on really well together. They instantly bonded and have become the best of friends.'

Nothing could obscure the fact, though, that there was an increasing level of love for Niall, and the acceleration all began in the United States of America. It took the American Directioners to see that the band was not all about Harry Styles: there were other members, too, and Niall was chief among them. Not that the rest of the band were lacking for fans, of course: more or less on touchdown in America, they found that they had a huge, fanatical and vocal following there. For Niall and Liam, both huge fans of America, this was particularly exciting. They were mobbed in Boston and, when they moved to Toronto in Canada, a crowd so huge and excitable surrounded their hotel that the police were called. The continent was going crazy for One Direction. While the fans stampeded in their direction, the media were not far behind.

The band were handed slots on primetime US shows, which treated them as pop royalty. Not only did One Direction get a slot on *Today*, the biggest breakfast television show in America, but they were trailed on the show not as some bunch of chancers from Britain and Ireland, but as a band akin to the Beatles. 'Now at 8.39 a.m., with the group that some people are saying are inspiring the next case of Beatlemania . . .' said the presenter. 'Odds are if you do have a teenager in your house, a pre-teen girl, she's already obsessed with One Direction.' The band duly appeared at the famous Rockefeller plaza, in the shadow of New York's iconic Rockefeller Center.

To the delight of fans, they arrived at the venue atop an open-top tourist bus. Niall was wearing a red shirt under a grey cardigan. He topped his outfit off with dark trousers and white high-top shoes. As the band lined up on the stage, he stood in the middle. Throughout the song ('What Makes You Beautiful') he pointed towards the camera at all the right moments, and did his increasingly customary air-drum rolls to punctuate the performance. This became quite a 'tick' of his both on television and on stage.

They also appeared on that other landmark US television

show, *Saturday Night Live*, in front of around 37 million viewers. 'This is our kind of show, you know. We like to have a bit of a laugh,' Niall told MTV ahead of the slot. 'This is our perfect kind of show – we get involved as much as we can,' he added of the comedic elements. He also tweeted about his excitement, writing, 'vocal lesson and warm up with @HeleneHorlyck in a while. Getting ready for SNL tonight! Gona be fun.'

Here, he stood on the far left of the line-up, wearing a short-sleeved white shirt. The studio audience screamed in all the right places and Niall fairly lapped up the adulation.

These were mammoth television slots. Hugely successful and established bands who had never quite made it onto either show could only look on with envy. Afterwards, Niall tweeted, 'SNL [*Saturday Night Live*] tonight was amazing. Thanks to @nbsnl for having us. Much appreciated!'

The publicity paid off in record sales. In February 2012, their debut single, 'What Makes You Beautiful', first charted in America at No. 28 – the highest *Billboard* Hot 100 debut by a UK act for fourteen years. Niall was in the back of a taxi cab when he learned of this news. He was en route to Sony Music to collect some tickets for a basketball game. 'My manager called me up and told me we were number one,' he told CKO196.9 Radio in Montreal, Canada. 'And I went crazy! I screamed my head off and the taxi driver nearly kicked me out of the car – he was freaked out!'

As Niall celebrated this news, little did he know that even better news was just around the corner: they had become first UK pop group to debut at No. 1 on the US *Billboard* album chart. The band were stunned and humbled by the news. Niall said, 'As you can imagine, we are over the moon'. Harry added on Digital Spy, 'We simply cannot believe that we are number one in America. It's beyond a dream come true for us. We want to thank each and every one of our fans in the US who bought our album and we would also like to thank the American public for being so supportive of us.'

Then it was time for their mentor – and surrogate uncle – Simon Cowell to express his pride. 'I couldn't be happier for One Direction, it is an incredible achievement,' he tweeted. Ever the canny operator, he added a tribute to the band's fan base, writing, 'They deserve it – they have the best fans in the world.'

A question frequently asked of One Direction's American success story is *why* and *how* they managed to conquer a pop market that so many other big British acts had failed even to dent. The roll call of top British and Irish acts who have failed to make a success of themselves Stateside is long. Among those who flopped there are Westlife, Robbie Williams and Oasis – some of the biggest names in the UK music scene in recent decades.

America has proved a graveyard for many British acts, who find it enormously demoralizing to move from being superstars in the UK to outsiders in the US. Busted, then Britain's biggest pop band and an act huge in Japan, even made an entertainingly tragic MTV documentary – called *America Or Busted* – recording their inability to make it in the States. With bands who had ruled the British charts for years failing in America, who could have held out hope for One Direction over there?

One man who did was Simon Cowell. The maestro had come close to American success with a previous British boy band he managed called 5ive. They had one reasonable hit in the States, called 'When the Lights Go Out'. However, the title proved prophetic and they faded soon afterwards. He said it was One Direction's distinctly *British* sound that made them a hit in the States. Too many acts before had tried to please both British and US audiences, which had made for a muddled image. 'I think with most of these bands, you end up with a sound that sounds somewhere between England and America – which means you fall smack down in the middle of the ocean,' he told *Rolling Stone*. 'You don't appeal to either.'

The forward planning for the US market that the One Direction management team undertook seems an obvious step to have made in hindsight. However, too many British bands in the past have been launched entirely with the UK market in mind. Cowell and the team had prepared more wisely – and how they reaped the benefits.

Another key factor in their popularity has been the harnessing of social media. As Justin Bieber showed during his meteoric rise, Twitter and YouTube are valuable weapons in the arsenal of a band's publicity team. This allows the band to penetrate quickly and widely, thanks to the greatest advocates of all: the fans. Rather than a handful of powerful media figures determining which acts get noticed and which do not, the public can now vote themselves by clicking the share buttons on their social networking accounts. Cowell could hardly believe how easily it all happened. 'Oh, my God, it was incredible,' he said in *Rolling Stone*. 'I remember years ago we had to do something on Disney.' Instead, Twitter, Facebook and YouTube were doing the job for him. Before One Direction were launched in the States he was being approached in America by girls who were already dedicated fans of the band. 'When I was out in America doing the auditions for *The X Factor*, everywhere I went there were blocks of One Direction fans going, "When are you going to bring this band to America?"'

He enjoyed the more organic process by which Niall's band were launched. 'Normally, we hassle the American labels when we think something is going to work,' he told

Rolling Stone. 'This time we said, "Let's just wait for the phone to ring and see who phones first." I wanted them to find out about the group first in a more buzzy way rather than us forcing the band on them.

'The band has to make it happen by themselves,' he said. 'I think that's what One Direction did. We worked as a partnership, but without their input and the way they spoke to the fans and the kind of people they are, it wouldn't have happened in the way that it's happening now.'

One of Cowell's key colleagues, Sonny Takhar, MD of Syco, joined Cowell in his appreciation of all things social. 'Sometimes you feel the song's the star, but it's not like that here – it's the act,' he said. 'It's a real moment,' added Takhar. 'Social media has become the new radio, it's never broken an act globally like this before.'

In addition to the factors outlined by Cowell and Takhar, we shouldn't forget that the American market had a yawning gap for a new boy band. Bands such as New Kids on the Block, the Backstreet Boys and *N Sync had never been fully replaced there. Even the Jonas Brothers, who in any case inhabited a slightly different part of the market, had long since enjoyed their peak. One Direction and their fellow British boy band the Wanted came along at just the right time.

So, One Direction's Stateside success can be explained

by a potent combination of charm and timing: they arrived as a new method of marketing was in its ascendancy and when the market itself was craving an act like them. And the different approach to One Direction's image informs the whole package. 'We're trying to do something different from what people would think is the typical kind of boy band,' Niall told the *National Post*. 'We're trying to do different kinds of music and we're just trying to be ourselves, not squeaky clean.' He rejected the notion that, in the twenty-first century, a boy band had to be 'air grabs' and the entire band 'dressed in all one colour'.

The band's musical talent was noted and remarked on during their US tour – and Niall was singled out for particular praise by *Rolling Stone*. 'The stripped-down set both showed off Horan's ability to play guitar, as well as One Direction's admirable live vocals,' wrote Erica Futterman. 'There was no need to worry about a backing track or a bum note, a pleasant realization at a pop show.' Jane Stevenson of Canoe wrote that, in the midst of the hysteria of their fans, it was easy to miss that One Direction 'can all actually sing in concert'. Melody Lau of the *National Post* also wrote that they can 'actually sing'. Niall was beginning to receive the sort of recognition he had craved.

Further, the One Direction American success story must be placed within the context of a wider era of British success in the United States. They were not the only British boy band making a huge go of it in America. The Wanted were also proving a hit there: their single, 'Glad You Came', peaked at No. 4 on the *Billboard* Hot 100; they also reached No. 5 on the US iTunes chart after the cast of the TV series *Glee* performed their song this week. The trend also goes beyond pop stars themselves, taking in television personalities. *Weakest Link* presenter Anne Robinson, reality television king Simon Cowell, controversial journalist Piers Morgan and Birmingham-born comedian John Oliver have all enjoyed enormous popularity in the American television industry since the start of the new millennium. The winners of the 2011 series of *The X Factor*, the girl band Little Mix, have also enjoyed Top Five hits in the USA. Niall was lucky to be in the pop industry just at the right time for Stateside success.

But a potential nightmare for him and his band was lurking in America, too. Soon after they arrived there news broke that a US band, also called One Direction, were planning to sue over the use of their name by the British band. The US band's lawyer, Peter Ross, claimed in the *Hollywood Reporter* that the band and their management had been aware for a while of the name-clash issue. 'Rather than change their name or do anything to create confusion or avoid damage to our goodwill, they chose to press ahead and come on their tour,' Ross said. 'We've been in negotiations for a month to find a resolution. In our view, the negotiations weren't turning out to be very productive.'

Cowell's record label Syco in due course countersued the American 1D, and eventually the case was resolved amicably. A joint statement concluded, 'All of the parties involved are pleased with the resolution and wish each other success.' The 'other' One Direction announced their new name on Facebook. 'The California band formerly known as One Direction, whose albums are titled *The Light* and *Uncharted Shores*, will now be known as Uncharted Shores,' they wrote. The case was resolved, but Niall had experienced a taste of the bitter side of popularity.

Niall's mother Maura visited him for part of the US tour and was bursting with pride and admiration for her son. Naturally, his fame and success impressed her. However, she was just as impressed by the fact that Niall looked after her so well. He made sure she did not want for a thing and did not have to pay for anything the entire time she was there. 'I've never had that in my life,' she told the *Daily Mirror* later. Just fourteen years earlier she had brought her young son to America for his first major holiday. Now, here they were, in the States again – but this time *he* was taking *her* around. She found the experience 'mind-blowing'.

He was less impressed when he and Liam were aggressively

accosted by some fans in New York. During a rare day off, the pair decided to have a look round Manhattan together. Both had been there separately as children; now they would walk the streets together as pop stars. However, they were swamped by a mob of fans. According to reports, the overexcitable bunch ripped Liam's shirt, jostled with them both and struck Niall in the face. Both were profoundly shaken by the experience. Later, Niall tweeted: 'This is a complete joke . . . ridic . . . Day off, wanna chill.' Liam added, 'That wasn't even funny.' It was a reminder that the more intense their fame became, the more risk there was that something dangerous could happen.

If reports are to be believed, Niall and Liam shared another experience during the tour: a thorough ticking-off over the size of the phone bills they ran up. This was not just for calls and texts, but also for online activities, particularly social networking. An insider at Simon Cowell's Syco label told the *Daily Mirror*: 'Like most teenagers, the boys are obsessed with all things social media. They're also encouraged to tweet by management to keep them interacting with fans, but Niall and Liam in particular got pretty homesick during their travels and regularly called home.

'When the bills landed on their doormat, the guys were utterly stunned and slightly devastated thinking they'd have to fork out themselves. In the end they got called in for a meeting and given a lecture on finances, and how to handle their money'. The source added that the lecture was for Niall's and Liam's own good, as it was 'vital' their wealth did not 'go to their heads'.

Meanwhile, the boys were off to tour Australia and New Zealand. For Niall, this was exciting, as he has relatives in Australia. The mania followed the band Down Under: when they appeared on Australian television, hundreds of fans flocked to stand outside the studio and scream their love for them. Niall apologized on Twitter to the fans who had flocked to the airport, as the band were unable to spend time with them. 'Australia, we're here. Sorry we couldn't come out, airport police said it wasn't safe. We really wanted to come out and say hi, cya soon.'

His bandmates were just as stunned. They had not expected the girls to be so excited on the other side of the planet. 'This is mental, it's absolutely incredible and we can't believe it,' said Liam in the *Telegraph* when he and his bandmates saw the scenes. The hysteria was such that the police had their work cut out to maintain order. One fan said she would be willing to be shot by a stun gun to get close to Niall and the other four heartthrobs. 'I'll do anything to see them, I'd even get tasered for this,' she said. 'I don't care, I just have to see them.' Niall did his best to maintain calm in his Twitter communication with the Oz Directioners, but all the hysteria did little to calm the nerves Niall sometimes felt over fans' intensity. One Direction made such an impact Down Under that, when tickets went on sale for their eighteen shows to be held there in September 2013, all 190,000 were instantly snapped up.

Country by country, One Direction were conquering the world.

A landmark moment in 'Directionmania' took place while the band were in Australia – and Niall was at the centre of it. During an appearance on the breakfast show *Sunrise*, Niall was encouraged to try the popular Australian sandwich spread Vegemite for the first time. Each member of the band had been invited to try an Aussie foodstuff for the first time. Zayn nibbled on a Pineapple Lump, Louis Tomlinson tried some Caramello chocolate, Liam ate some Tim-Tams biscuits, while Harry Styles ate a meat pie. However, when Niall came to try Vegemite he was so unimpressed he spat it back into his hand.

Afterwards, Niall, who had been missing Irish sausages and English tea throughout their overseas travels, wrote on Twitter: 'Can clearly say vegemite is horrible! Like tryin new stuff though.'

What happened next summed up how popular the band were and how far their fans would go to get close to them. The half-eaten piece of toast left behind by Niall was put up for auction on eBay, where it attracted almost $100,000 (£65,000) in online bids. The broadcaster itself opened the auction, with the proceeds set for the Australian charity YoungCare. The eBay listing notes, 'The item is perishable and although we will package it so that tampering is evident, we do not advise that it is consumed. We will not be including the mouthful that Niall spat out – because that's just gross.'

Niall's obsession with food and drink have become a charming feature of his public image. Most famously, he adores the high-street chains Wagamama and Nando's. However, he also likes more simple, homespun stuff such as tea, which he always drinks a certain way. He told CBS Radio: 'Back home we call it a "builder's tea" – it's like really strong tea, loads of milk, loads of sugar so basically you can stand your spoon up in it. It's that strong.'

His obsession with food is worth reflecting on, too. Asked during an interview on 94.7 Fresh FM what his strategy would be to win the game featured in the *Hunger Games* movie, he replied, 'I'd give up 'cos I'd get too hungry early; I'd probably die straightaway.' He often tweets about his

151

food, often with a humorous angle. Posting a photograph of empty items of crockery, he added the caption, 'Niall VS Food! Haha I win.' He has often been the victor in such battles; however, he has also suffered defeats after eating the wrong food. On a flight during their world tour, he tweeted that he was 'not feeling the best'. Later, he got to the source of his discomfort, tweeting, 'Food poisoning not good'.

Not good at all. Indeed, while there were so many fun times on the road for Niall there were also some very painful moments. For instance, one day on the 2013 world tour, he and the band's tour manager, Paul Higgins, were having a bit of a playful scrap when Higgins's watch caught Niall's hand and cut his thumb. And Niall had come within inches of injury when a fan had thrown a bizarre projectile at him during a concert in America. While performing in Houston, Texas, Niall had noticed something flying through the air towards him. It turned out to be an iPhone, with a house key and a lurid letter attached to it. Due to the brightness of the stage lights Niall noticed only at the very last moment,. He managed to knock it clear just before it injured him. On a different occasion a fan threw one half of a walkie-talkie set onto the stage, in the hope that one of the band would pick it up and talk to her. Niall was heartily impressed by the enterprise of it all. The Directioners rarely fail to make him smile.

It had been a wonderful experience for Niall to tour overseas and to see the reactions of thousands and thousands of fans. Yet, on his return to Ireland, he landed with a metaphorical bump. As he arrived in Dublin Airport, a group of fans were waiting for him. This was by now a familiar part of life for Niall, as was the fact they were filming him on their mobile phones. So perhaps he should have known better than to do what we did next. Niall is normally very well drilled when it comes to speaking to the band's fans, almost invariably adding in the sort of sentiments that fans crave to hear from their heroes. Yet on this occasion, he was caught on camera swearing at a group of girls who were waiting for him.

It was not long before it was spreading throughout the Internet. Despite the fact that the fans who filmed the footage seemed to be untroubled by his words, some who saw the video said that Niall had meant the statement offensively. Indeed, the term he used is often said by younger Irish people as one of bantering affection. Still, he should perhaps have known better. He took to Twitter to clear up the mess, writing, 'Really sorry if I caused any offence. It was just banter with fans who I think of more as mates. But I understand that it's not a word I should be using at all.' It was a lesson learned for Niall – and for his bandmates, who observed the controversy aghast.

The truth was that the band were entering a third chapter

in their development. First had been *The X Factor* era, in which they had been assembled by and had then competed in the famous television talent show. Then came the initial wave of fame, during which they could do no wrong as far as the media were concerned. Everyone was too busy trying to attract a few motes of the One Direction magic dust to find anything negative in their almost fairytale ascendancy in Britain and Ireland, as well as further afield. However, having built the band up, some elements of the media were preparing themselves to knock them down. The favoured, if unpleasant, tendency of the press remains alive and well. For those who delight in knocking people off their perch, there were few more prized targets than Niall and One Direction. All members would have to tread carefully, as Niall had learned, and demonstrated, afresh during the Dublin Airport 'swearing at fans' controversy.

The peril was complicated by the fact that the sense of backlash the band were facing coincided with a renewed sense of rebellion *within* the band. Like all pop acts, the band were forced to a degree to conform to the demands of their management and record label. This meant they were handed a relentless workload and were expected to adopt a 'safe' image. For the most part, the band seemed happy to go along with what was asked of them, but moments of rebellion did leak out. Liam wrestled back an element of individuality when he had his much-loved locks shaved off, leaving him closely cropped.

'At the start, the management said I wasn't allowed to change my hair,' he told *Vogue*. 'But then I did it anyway, so they kind of let that one go.' Suddenly, he was able to walk around the streets of Britain and America without being recognized. One day, he donned a decoy outfit – he was 'dressed as a big chav – Adidas trainers, jogging bottoms', he said – and walked around revelling in his newfound anonymity. Naturally, as his new hairstyle became recognizable, his period of relative personal serenity passed. He had so enjoyed it; it was something the other band members, Niall included, found themselves craving.

The media were watching the band closely for any cracks in either their happiness and unity or their behaviour. Even when Niall was not directly involved in incidents, they had a knock-on effect on him by association. Sometimes, in truth, the band are complicit, stoking the media fire. In November 2012, for instance, members of One Direction engaged in a Twitter spat with members of the rival boy band the Wanted. It was an adult exchange that saw Zayn Malik dub the Wanted's Max George as 'chlamydia boy'. In response, George implied that Zayn was a marijuana user, tweeting, 'Stay off the bud . . . It clearly makes u cranky.'

This made for a public-relations challenge for the band's

handlers. While the band have never been presented as angelic or whiter than white, all concerned with One Direction's image are conscious that a whiff of alleged drug abuse gives a less than ideal message to the band's youngest fans. It also increases the pressure on the band from the media, as photographers sense a chance for a new 'money shot'. As for Zayn, he has never admitted to any use of drugs. Indeed, one of his bandmates has actively denied that any of One Direction have touched narcotics. Asked about drugs during a press conference in Madrid, Louis said, 'We don't need any of that. We'll just stick to the Pepsi!' It was a reassuring return to a more wholesome place for the band, and Niall had done well to stay out of this particular controversy.

Enough of the *engineered* drama. In August 2012, Niall was struck with *genuine* drama and bereavement when one of his friends from Ireland was killed in a car crash. Quentin Reilly, from Niall's hometown of Mullingar, died in hospital from injuries he suffered in the single-vehicle smash. All three men involved had been taken to hospital. On learning of the tragedy, Niall wrote on Twitter, 'Hope the lads make a full recovery, also Quentin will be missed. Thoughts with the Reilly family at this time.'

Fans of One Direction were quick to offer their hero their condolences. For him, the fact that private tragedies will be played out publicly is a fact of life. The loss of someone he knew was a reminder for Niall that, for all that his life was now lived in something of a bubble, 'real life' outside continued, with all the wonderful and horrendous truths that entailed.

A happier occasion came when the band celebrated its own second birthday. Niall tweeted, 'Guys its been 2 years today since we were formed, its been incredible so far, its all down to you guys! Love you all soo much! Thank you.'

A few weeks later, Niall and Liam gave some of their London-based fans a pleasant surprise when they made an impromptu appearance at the Westfield shopping centre. They appeared unannounced at the Shepherds Bush mall, with Niall carrying an acoustic guitar. Wearing sunglasses and a back-to-front blue baseball cap, he looked very cool as he accompanied Liam for a stripped-down rendition of 'What Makes You Beautiful'. Westfield's house backing band, Soul Chango, provided some more music for them. Soon a crowd of surprised shoppers had surrounded the performers. Nobody could quite believe that two members of the world's biggest pop band were there, casually playing a low-key, unannounced 'gig' in the capital's famous shopping mall.

The summer gave Niall many thrills as he followed the London 2012 Olympic games, in which two people hailing from Niall's hometown were competing. Showjumper Josh Murphy and boxer John Joe Nevin were both from Mullingar. He even spoke to the boxer on the phone during the Olympics. 'He's a sound lad,' Niall tweeted after their chat. 'We grew up 100 yards away from each other, now he's goin for an olympic medal.'

Niall was now getting a taste of the sort of inspiration that other locals felt during his own rise to fame on *The X Factor*. As he had inspired other Irishmen and Irishwomen, so were other Irish folk inspiring him. Although he was annoyed when he overslept and missed a crucial Euro 2012 game for Ireland, Niall was back in a good place emotionally as the band put the finishing touches to their second album.

The band attended the wedding of James Corden, and, to Niall's embarrassment, he and Louis had arrived wearing identical outfits. Each had opted for a charcoal grey Kooples suit with a white shirt. Naturally, there was plenty of laughter and good-natured banter over the matter. Olympic diving star Tom Daley, one of dozens of other famous guests, even tweeted a photograph of them with the caption 'Yes – they are wearing the same suits!!! Haha.'

Niall need not have worried about the public attention that fell on him, because, as had so often been the case before and would be again, it was speculation over Harry's love life that grabbed the headlines the next day. Harry had been He was spotted flirting with the thirty-seven-year-old singer Natalie Imbruglia. The band also chatted with another Aussie soap star turned singer, the legendary Kylie Minogue. 'I was drinking with One Direction at [the] wedding,' she told the *Sunday Mirror*. 'I was hanging with the teens.' She advised Niall and the gang to take risks and learn who they are.

Niall had learned a great deal in the first two years of One Direction. He had slowly begun to come to terms with the hysterical reactions he prompted in young female fans around the world. His initial discomfort should not be viewed as in any way disapproving. He loves his fans back and is eternally grateful for their support; he acknowledges that the band would get nowhere without it. He had also learned more and more about the fame game: what to say in public and, just as importantly, what *not* to say in public. He and the band had enjoyed a breathless rise from *The X Factor* to global fame. They knew that, if anything, the fame and its pressures would only increase in the foreseeable future. Stars do not rise to the stunningly high levels that theirs had, only to crash immediately. Niall knew there was more excitement to come. Sometimes, it was true, it all frightened him. Mostly, however, he was thrilled and could hardly wait to see what happened next.

CHAPTER SIX

THIS IS US

It is never easy to get a debut album right. Here, musically, is the band's first chance to make a substantial musical statement to the world. It is their first big expression. With *Up All Night*, One Direction and their team had got it just right. The album had, in the eyes of most, helped them to the very top of the pop ladder. Following it up would be an even tougher task to get right, not least because they had set the bar so high with their debut. The band had been working with a string of musical talents, including McFly frontman Tom Fletcher. They had already been described as 'really likeable' by Fletcher, and it seemed the more they worked together the better they got on.

Niall tweeted a photo of Fletcher in the studio with One Direction. In his hands was his famous pink ukulele. Niall described the work he did with the McFly members on Twitter as a 'great session'. He quoted approvingly the words of McFly's Danny Jones: 'If we can't write a song, we'll have a laugh!' Whether the band were joined by outsiders or not, Niall almost invariably loved their time in the studio working on the follow-up to *Up All Night*. 'What a sick day in the studio!' he tweeted on one occasion. 'Got loads of vocal down and recorded 2 songs! On guitar!' On another occasion, he announced, 'I'm lying on my bunk on the bus outside a recording studio, thinking, we're recording album 2 already!'

The truth was that Niall was not only sending these messages to share his excitement and enthusiasm. He was also trying to make a point. He had been stung by the perception that the band was an entirely manufactured unit, its members mere putty in the hands of executives. So around this time he began to make plenty of noise about the input he was having. 'The way it works for us, I don't know how everyone else works, but people don't see the meetings that we do, the all-day meetings about the album, and the way the songs are going to be even listed on the back of the album and album artwork,' he told MTV.

Harry, too, has sounded his note. 'We're always writing on the road and in hotels and airports,' he said. 'We don't ever want our music to sound like a forty-year-old man in an office has written it and given it to us to perform.' Niall added, 'We want to have the most control we possibly can of everything that we do. Like at the moment, I'm just proofreading the single artwork for the next single. They don't see that.'

While his words would not satisfy all of the 'they' he was aiming them at, his point was made as well as it could be. To an extent, if One Direction are to enjoy longevity, it will depend on their being allowed to have increasing creative input – or at least give the impression that this is the case. After all, while a band are still in their teens and new to the fame game, they're likely to accept situations that their hardened, worldly-wise, twentysomething selves of the future will find embarrassing.

The first single to be released from the second album was 'Live While We're Young'. 'It's a little different from what we've heard before – but when you're the world's biggest boy band, it's no bad thing,' wrote *Digital Spy*. Yet, in truth, the song was little different from the band's previous sound. Mikael Wood wrote in the *Los Angeles Times* that it was a 'characteristically peppy piece of high-gloss party pop', while MSN Music's Tina Hart called it a 'massive pop win . . . it's fun, pure unadulterated pop and I like it.' The video, too, garnered praise. Shot in Tunbridge Wells, Kent, it shows them having a jolly, caper-filled day out. An 'epic summer adventure', purred the *Huffington Post*. It reached No. 1 in the UK and in the US it shifted 341,000 copies in the first week and reached the top of the charts.

Then it was time for the album. Liam had admitted that the band felt a lot of pressure as the album was prepared for release. 'It's the second-album syndrome thing – or whatever they call it,' he said in the *Daily Star*. He added that the band hoped *Take Me Home* would sound more 'live' than *Up All Night*. It got its name after lengthy consideration, as Niall explained. 'We thought about it for a while,' he said on Ryan Seacrest's KIIS-FM show, 'because we all do a lot of travelling around the world and we get to see a lot of cool places, but the main thing is there's no place like home. It's always kind of nice to go home.'

The album cover featured Niall in a red telephone box. Liam is draped over the top of the box while an ever-enthusiastic Louis is climbing up, supported by Zayn. As for Harry, he stands to one side observing the fun, his arms folded and a not uncharacteristic air of self-satisfaction about him. There would be surprises for the fans on the album, yet it opened in familiar tone. 'Live While We're Young' is similar in many ways to the opener of *Up All*

Night, 'What Makes You Beautiful'. The opening guitar riff immediately captures the attention and the song itself, a fine summery youth anthem, does not disappoint. The tempo increases more in the second track, 'Kiss You'. It is a breathless romp and a very catchy three minutes of pop. For as long as it appears on the set list of One Direction live shows, Niall and the guys will have to keep fit in order to perform its fast, potentially tongue-tying lyrics. The phrase 'take me home' from the chorus would be used as the title of their next tour.

Then comes the album's first departure from the band's previous material, and one that Niall was personally delighted they took. Co-written by the legendary Ed Sheeran and Fiona Bevan, 'Little Things' is like nothing the band had recorded before. It is a gentle acoustic ballad with a lyric that expresses emotional depths the band had never previously hinted at. Niall noticed how the success of 'Little Things' saw their fanbase widen both in number and demographic variety. 'It's broadening the audience for sure,' he told *Billboard*. 'I get a lot of dudes, a lot of moms and dads coming up and saying they love it.' (Sheeran, who is a close friend of the band, also wrote another of the album's tracks, the less memorable 'Over Again'.) For Niall, forever toting his beloved acoustic guitars, this song is a favourite. He's become very emotional while singing it on occasion.

'Last First Kiss' is a more uptempo, but still definitely mature, ballad, though of a heavier hue than 'Little Things'. The choppy, staccato 'Change My Mind' is, both musically and lyrically, another track that would have been too mature for their debut album. Yet it sits comfortably enough on *Take Me Home*. The chorus is a call to arms, characteristic of the new mood. In 'Back for You', the comparatively innocent boys of the *Up All Night* era hint at more adult and raunchy intentions with the ever-present female characters of their music. It is safe to say that, judging by the unflinching suggestions that thousands of fans tweet to the boys each day, few of their fans were to be offended by the song, which Louis has described in music news website Billboard as feeling 'quite band-y'.

The clapping beat at the start of 'Rock Me' is reminiscent of 1970s rock legends Queen's song 'We Will Rock You'. Given the close similarity in the drumbeat and the echo of 'Rock' in the title, the resemblance is surely an intentional mini-tribute. For the second album running, a track written by McFly is included to the delight of fan Niall, this time in the shape of 'I Would'. The song would cause a controversy when, during an interview with the *Metro* newspaper, McFly suggested they had palmed One Direction off with some inferior material. McFly frontman Danny Jones said that his bandmate Tom Fletcher had sent One Direction a 'slightly s**tter' song. The story created quite a storm and Fletcher was quick to issue a denial, stating it was 'obviously completely false' and that Jones had only been joking.

Several tracks included songs written by the band themselves. Niall and the other members found that their most productive sessions were not as a five, but when some members were elsewhere. 'It was actually usually groups of three,' said Liam. 'It's nice to have two people around. When you have more than two people working together it gets a bit unfocused as an idea.'

Niall loved the creativity of it all. These songwriting sessions, and those of the band's talented creative contacts, had produced a fine set of pop tunes that built into a memorable and well-received album. Rather than being a churned-out carbon copy of the first album, *Take Me Home* took the band into new areas. At this rate, their third album, due in late 2013, could be a fascinating prospect.

Meanwhile, the reviews for *Take Me Home* were largely positive. The *Independent* declared it to be 'sing-into-your-hairbrush, life-enhancing pop', which 'has "OMG!!!!" written all over it'. The *Boston Globe* deemed it 'uniformly sleek and upbeat', while *Rolling Stone* preferred the heavier tracks to the lighter efforts, declaring that the Take Me Home album 'rivals the best of Backstreet and *N Sync when the material pumps'. However, the influential US mag said that elsewhere that 'a certain amount of douchiness creeps in'. Commercially, there was no such equivocation: the album was another solid smash hit. It reached No. 1 in a staggering thirty-five countries, including the UK, USA, Canada and Australia. Those cynics who had insisted One Direction would be a one-hit wonder were forced to revise their sour verdicts. Incredibly, the already-huge boy band were actually growing in popularity as their career continued.

The album's release and reception was a high in December 2012 for Niall. However, the highlight of the year for him (and for most American Directioners) came at New York's landmark venue, Madison Square Garden. Only the very elite of the world of pop have performed at the iconic venue. For each member of the band, particularly Niall, who both loves and is loved by America, this was a special moment. Liam was thrilled too. As Niall and the others crouched backstage, waiting to walk in front of the twenty-thousand-strong audience, they could hardly believe they were playing there. The fact that they had sold out the venue within sixty seconds of the tickets going on sale only swelled their pride – and their pre-show anxiety.

Louis had been nervous that their rehearsals for the show might not have been sufficiently thorough. Niall had

had his scared moments as well. It all went well on the night, though, and throughout the pulsating performance the band remarked on their excitement. 'I'm overwhelmed,' Zayn told the screaming fans. 'I'm from a small town in Bradford. Things like this don't happen to people like me.' As for Niall, he put it best when he said, 'This is the best night of our lives. You guys have travelled from all around the world and we cannot believe what has happened here tonight.' His buddy Ed Sheeran joined them on stage for their rendition of 'Little Things' and, by the time they crowned the encore with their debut hit 'What Makes You Beautiful', they had New York in the palms of their hands. Later, they partied the night away at the Hudson Hotel.

What a year Niall was having! Some had 'predicted' that the end of the world would occur in 2012, but instead his band were ruling much of Planet Pop. Their debut album continued to sell ferociously, ultimately reaching the top of the charts in more than sixteen countries. Its successor would hit the top in more than twice as many territories. The Fantastic Five's popularity and influence was soaring, and with it their profits: by June 2012, their business empire, which stretched across the globe, was worth $50 billion. The band became almost a mini-industry in their own right: the immediate team specifically employed to look after One Direction, including managers, stylists and producers, was ninety-strong. With their success in the all-important American market growing all the time, it was expected that their profits would continue to soar in the years ahead, with their record label confidently predicting they would double their income in 2013.

Music retailer HMV reported that One Direction's official calendar for 2013 was outselling those of Justin Bieber and that young man of the moment, Olympic diver Tom Daley. For instance, in October, they reached *Heat* magazine's rich list of young stars, thanks to their estimated collective personal fortunes of £26.33 million. (Niall was once asked what he would do if he were Simon Cowell for a day. He answered that he would spend £20 million in one day, just because he could. He was also asked how he would spend his last day on earth. He answered that he would go for a pint with Ronan Keating.)

With the money flooding in as a result of their singles, albums, concerts and other music-related activities, the band and their team set up some non-musical activities to boost their coffers even further. The first such project was the filming of a One Direction movie. Following the example of Canadian pop prince Justin Bieber's enormously successful film *Never Say Never*, they decided that *One Direction: This Is Us* would be filmed in 3D. It would be directed by Morgan Spurlock, best known for his work on the fast-food documentary *Super Size Me*. The director described the new project in suitably awed tones as an 'epic undertaking'. Simon Cowell told *Digital Spy* that the film was for the fans to honour how they 'have made history around the world'.

Niall has, from the start, been the band member most excited by the project. He promised MTV that the film would give a chance for the fans to get more intimate with the boys. He said the intention was to 'get our personalities across' so their fans can 'get to know us deeper'. Niall was handed a video camera, so he could record some raw footage to add to the mix. Harry feels the film will be a great personal document, which will be of interest for future generations of the Styles family. 'Just to have the ability to be able to kind of look back at that while we're older and to have your children see it will be amazing,' he said.

Just as some people have suggested that the band mime on stage, so did some commentators wonder whether the movie was scripted. Louis insisted this was not the case. 'No, nothing at all was scripted,' he told *Total Film* magazine. 'You know if we are asked the questions . . . we just answer naturally. Because I think that's the most important part, that we show people who we are. And you know, to do that we can't have anything scripted. So it's all a reality.'

Niall attempted to smooth the question over. 'It's more documentary than concert,' he told RTÉ Two in 2013. 'It's just a bit of insight into what goes on. You can imagine fans standing outside arenas, wondering what goes on in the dressing room. I think this is what we want them to see because the fans know us but they know the public perception,' he added. 'I think it's good for them to see what we're like as people and friends.'

In June, he watched the final cut of the film and then sent some emotional messages to his followers on Twitter. 'Just watched a cut of "This is us"! Made me look at life so differently! man I love you guys! You've changed our lives!' He added, 'by the way you're gona wana see the movie when it comes . . .'

In June, they followed in the steps of Justin Bieber, Jennifer Lopez, Britney Spears and Lady Gaga by launching their own perfume, called 'Our Moment'. At the launch, held in London's 'Gherkin' building, the lads described the perfume as 'vibrant and playful, fruity floral', having put together pink grapefruit, wild berries, redcurrants, jasmine, freesia, musk and patchouli. The anchor for the launch was the Irish presenter Laura Whitmore, a good friend of Niall's. Niall quipped that he had already road-tested the scent on his family. 'I had a little tester bottle and my mam is a big fan, so that's all my Christmas presents cleared up,' he said.

Harry added that the creation of the scent had been a 'long and exciting process'. However, the biggest noise about the scent came when the band released their promotional video for it. The forty-one-second black-and-white video features the boys playing around to a background of gentle acoustic guitar. Niall's looks work particularly well in the monochrome, but the biggest talking point of the video is, inevitably, when Harry playfully kisses Zayn.

Despite these departures, the focus was never far from what Niall loved most – the music. He would soon get a chance to unveil yet more dates for his favourite part of life in a band – live performance, because, during the summer, the band also announced yet another tour, and this one would be bigger than anything they had embarked on or arranged before. In 2014, Niall and the band would set out on a worldwide stadium tour. 'We are ecstatic,' said Niall at the press conference at Wembley Stadium in London. 'We've only been a band for three years and we're already doing stadiums – including Wembley.' Given the international nature of the tour, Liam had a cheeky suggestion for Niall. 'I think it would be quite interesting to sing a song in Spanish,' he said. 'Niall can sing "The Lion King" in Spanish!' The frenetic nature of their schedule was made clear as the band left the press conference. Having announced one global tour, they jetted straight off to continue their current one. Switzerland – and Zurich – beckoned.

At their initial announcement, they unveiled the first thirteen dates which included an appearance in the Irish capital, in the form of the 82,300-seater GAA stadium in Dublin's Croke Park. Indeed, it would be in Ireland that the European leg of the tour would begin. Niall, who has never made any secret of his dream to play at Croke Park one day, was so excited. 'Please don't be disappointed if your country wasn't announced,' he urged his Twitter followers. 'We will be announcing more over the year!' He also tweeted, 'For us this is absolutely crazy! We are soo excited! Every night is just gona be amazing ! You're support is incredible you have done this x.'

Industry experts quickly estimated Niall and his bandmates could pocket €10 million or more each from the tour, once ticket sales, extra dates and merchandising are taken into account. There was a charitable element to the tour, however. For the UK and Ireland dates, 50 pence from the sale of each ticket would be donated to the Stand Up To Cancer charity. Liam spoke for the band when he said, 'Stand Up To Cancer is all about bringing people together as a collective force and we hope our fans will get involved too. We'd love for One Direction fans to tell us about their support by using the hashtag #1DStandUp.' Stand Up To

Cancer was expected to receive approximately £200,000 from the sales.

A second date at Croke Park was quickly added. A stadium tour is always a huge undertaking for a band. While the venues were chosen carefully based on demand for the past tours the band had done, there can still be a sense of anxiety as the tickets are about to go on sale. The tour was named 'Where We Are', and all involved with One Direction hoped very much that stadiums were, in terms of ticket demand, where they were. Will the stadiums prove to be that bit too large for the band's fanbase? Or will the tickets sell out within minutes, as with the previous theatre and arena tours? Sure enough, Directionmania continued and saw the tickets greedily snapped up within minutes of the on-sale time. Niall was thrilled, and tweeted his bandmates, describing their fans in gushing terms. He wrote, '@real_liam_payne @louis_tomlinson @zaynmalik @harry_styles we simply have the best fans in the world boys! Without a doubt!'

In fact, if some staggering research by a ticketing firm was anywhere near accurate, then there had never been a question that the dates would sell out in super-fast time. According to data complied by the ticketing website Seatwave, one in five of the UK's teenagers attempted to get a ticket to one of the shows. 'We all know One Direction are incredibly huge right now. However, to imagine that one in every five teens will be vying for One Direction tickets is truly mind boggling,' Louise Mullock, spokesperson for Seatwave, said in the *Daily Mirror*. 'They really are the biggest music act on the planet right now.'

Niall had come so far and so much had happened to him. Sometimes, when he got a moment to catch his breath and reflect, he wondered what on earth was round the corner for him next.

CHAPTER SEVEN

THE PRICE OF FAME

Fame is a seductive yet volatile beast. It brings so much excitement, joy, wealth and so much else to be thrilled about. Yet it also brings less pleasant things, including intrusion, and takes away some precious things, not least privacy. These things are not limited to the famous themselves: many of them also affect those around the celebrity – their family, friends and, most pertinently here, their lovers. Celebrity is a fearsome whirlwind that whips into its midst the willing and the less willing. Naturally, the more intense the fame, the more exciting and frightening all of this is. Few twenty-first-century celebrities have faced more intense fame than Niall and One Direction. For all the joys and gifts this has brought Niall and those near him, at times it has also come with a bitter price.

At the end of 2012, Niall reportedly started dating a twenty-year-old drama student called Amy Green. She was said to have broken off a former relationship in order to be with Niall, whom she met at a London nightclub. He apparently worked hard to 'woo' the pretty Green, but the relationship fell apart within months. It had hit the rocks when she began to find Niall too immature and inexperienced romantically. 'It was like Niall's first relationship, whereas Amy had been in a relationship before,' a 'source' told the *Sun*. Then, with Niall's schedule becoming ever more demanding, they simply drifted apart.

The source continued, 'Sadly, it is over between Niall and Amy. He finished it because he didn't have enough time with everything he has to do. Understandably, she was disappointed because she had been in a relationship before she started seeing Niall and chose him over her boyfriend. But there are no real hard feelings and they're still close.'

It could have ended happily there, were it not for the fact that Green was already receiving nasty messages from Niall's fans long before the split.

Like many a young lady who has been linked with One Direction, Green was soon the subject of an upsettingly intense tide of online abuse. As soon as she had been linked with Niall, she began to be bombarded with unpleasant messages on Twitter. Even after they split, Green continued to receive upsetting tweets. She also found some of the press reports about their relationship distressing, and took to Twitter to vent her own feelings. 'Where do some people get their facts from?!! . . . very funny,' she wrote. She then retweeted a message her sister Georgia had posted, reading, 'Laughing at what people will say to make an article #hysterical #getyourfactsright.'

This was far from the first time such a state of affairs had come about. When Harry was romantically involved with television host Caroline Flack for a while, she received a huge amount of abuse. After feeling sickened by the flood of threats and vitriol she was facing, she sent a message out in response. 'Hi one direction fans! To clarify. I'm close friends with Harry. He's one of the nicest people I know . . . I don't deserve death threats :) x.' The fact that she even had to make the last point spoke volumes for what she had been facing. Even after the couple split, the envy of some fans was not assuaged, prompting Harry to tweet in defence of Caroline. 'She is one of the kindest, sweetest people I know. Please respect that.'

His experience with Green aside, Niall has been largely a bystander in the trend but has watched horrified as it became ever more clear that a sizeable number of One Direction fans are willing and able to make life hell for any girl who gets close to any member of the band. Liam's on/off girlfriend Danielle Peazer had received some unpleasant messages over the years. Even Hannah Walker, a gentle blonde who was dating Louis long before he became famous, was ruthlessly targeted on Twitter. So horrified and upset did she become by the what she faced that she ended up taking prolonged 'breaks' from social networking.

This was a perpetually smouldering issue but occasionally it ignited into something more fierce. For instance, in April 2012 a twenty-year-old woman said she had been 'bullied' online into cancelling a date with Zayn. Anna Crotti had met him during the band's stay in Australia. 'A security guard came up to me. I thought I was in trouble but he said, "The lads want your number,"' she told MTV. 'I got a text later saying hello. I asked who it was and it was Zayn.'

Word soon spread that she was speaking with Zayn, and that was when the trouble started. 'By the end of the day, it got a bit too scary,' she said. 'Random girls were abusing me on Facebook. Girls were calling the radio station and giving me s**t. Mothers even called me in tears, demanding to know if I knew where One Direction were because their daughters wanted to meet them. I didn't even want to walk home. It was so intense. I messaged Zayn and said, "Maybe it's not a good idea we meet up." It was just a bit too full on.'

This trend has left Niall and the others in a contradictory position. On the one hand, these famous, good-looking, rich young men are very desirable as boyfriend material. However, at the same time they are also a terrifying proposition. Who would want to throw themselves at the mercy of online hate mobs by dating one of the band? Louis showed that his patience was wearing ever thinner when he confronted his fans on Twitter. He discovered that, under the hashtag 'Louannah' – a nickname used during his relationship with Hannah Walker – fans had been tweeting his girlfriend, Eleanor Calder, with photographs of him with Walker. He was furious and took to Twitter to make his feelings known. In a particularly frank outburst, he wrote, 'Truth of the matter is its actually not funny in the slightest. I'm reading through some horrible tweets very p*ssed off!' He also sent a message directly to Calder, reassuring her of his feelings: 'Love YOU! xxxx'; and then he added, 'I couldn't be happier right now, so let it be :) Thank youuuuu x.' He knew that his fans would see the message, so it was as much aimed at them as it was addressed to Calder herself.

These incidents had been an eye-opening experience for Niall and the rest of the band. As 2013 dawned, Niall was already well versed in the ways of fame after a crash course in celebrity since the band formed. Given the pace of that course, there were still parts of being a famous figure that he was still coming to terms with. Crowds were one of them. Massive, manic crowds of fans seemed to follow the band wherever they went. Terrifying scenes of the boys being swamped by aggressively excited mobs of girls became worryingly commonplace. No wonder Niall, who can suffer from bouts of claustrophobia, felt frightened at times. He admitted after just one year in the band that it was proving to be a 'slow process' to come to terms with the pressure of the fan's love for him and the rest of the band. 'Obviously, when I was at school I never had hundreds of girls screaming at me,' he said in an ITV2 documentary on the band.

These moments created a dilemma for Niall. He wanted to speak out about what the band were facing in such scenarios and the peculiar way it troubled him. Yet he and the band were mindful that these mobs comprised the band's fans. Therefore, a straightforward condemnation of their behaviour would be unwise. He trod the path carefully, showing again his awareness of the ways of cool public relations. 'I'm quite claustrophobic and I don't like everyone crowding around and shouting the same questions,' he confessed to *We Love Pop* magazine. 'I get a little bit scared sometimes. It's all good as we've got a good security team.'

The band had suffered a series of injuries and ailments in recent months, making each member even more aware of the need for safety. Niall, as we saw in Chapter 2, dislocated his knee on fourteen occasions. Harry, meanwhile, had a persistent bad back, for which he was taking Pilates classes. Zayn had been on crutches for a while after hurting himself at a party. Liam had broken his toe after dropping a laptop computer on it. As performers, the band had to stay in tiptop physical condition. Anything, even fans, that threatened that tended to freak them out. With *Rolling Stone* magazine noting that the management were working them 'like dogs', fears grew that the band might be headed for trouble.

Indeed, in 2013 the pressures of his fame began to tell on Niall. In June, he sent a series of tweets complaining about his lot, as the *Take Me Home* tour hit its American leg. 'AC [air conditioning] in hotel rooms is horrible! Makes your throat real dry! Just slept all night with it on!' he wrote. He then expressed how deeply he craved normality. More than anything he wanted to be left alone for a while so he could relax. 'Stalked out of it!' he wrote, adding, 'Wish I could just chill on the day off. I'm tired today!'

Earlier, he had headed to the pool at the band's Miami hotel and was quickly swamped by excited fans. With press photographers also following his every move, Niall could be forgiven for feeling freaked out. Prior to his fame, he could only have dreamed of being jetted around the world, staying in luxury hotels in Florida. Yet these perks came with a price. Had he remained an ordinary teenager in Ireland, he would have been free to walk wherever he wanted, with no intrusions or pressure. Niall's claustrophobia and cool were sorely tested by such mobbing. Although the next day he returned to the pool, where he frolicked with a buff-looking Harry, the hurt apparent in his words was hard to miss.

Niall was not the first to break from the official party line. The previous year, during an interview in America for *NOW* magazine, Liam had expressed a yearning for his former, simpler life. 'It's all happening so fast, it's hard to take it all in,' he began. 'Sometimes it's only when I'm on my own that I think about everything and sometimes I think I would quite like to just go home. There's a part of me that occasionally wants to go back to Wolverhampton and just chill out, play the field, be normal again. It's a catch-22 situation, I guess.'

There had also been several reports (including one from Perez Hilton) suggesting that Zayn was 'on the brink' of leaving the band owing to his growing discomfort in the public spotlight. However, it was Niall's statements that stood out most strongly, because they formed the biggest contrast with his usually affable and compliant mood. He has always been a smooth talker in terms of public relations, ever mindful of toeing the line. So, while his statement was not the stuff of front-page scandal, it did raise eyebrows. Were the band's colossal fame and breathless work rate pushing its members too far?

The speculation was hardly dampened when a solo song, recorded by Harry, leaked online. The sweet ballad, 'Don't Let Me Go', had just the sort of added layer of maturity and poise that one would imagine would accompany a bid for solo stardom by Harry. Was he preparing to jump ship? A spokesperson for One Direction insisted this was not the case. 'It was a demo they worked on over a year ago that was being considered for a One Direction song,' said the spokesperson, quoted in the *Daily Mail*. 'Sometimes the boys write and record separately as they work on new material, but this is not a solo release.'

At the same time it was revealed that each band member had set up an individual publishing deal to capitalize on his songwriting credits. They each signed a deal with the song-publishing company Fingate, who also look after the back catalogues of Elvis Presley, Britney Spears and Foo Fighters. Niall was excited to sign his deal, not least because it offered him another chance to demonstrate that he was not putty in the hands of the band's handlers, but rather a creative spark in his own right.

'This is a real statement of intent from the band,' a 'source' told the *Sun*. 'They have absolutely no intention of being spoon-fed pop puppets. They want to write and they want to earn as individuals.' Each member of the group had also set up a personal recording studio in his own home to work on new music. Yet the focus remained on Harry's solo song – and the subsequent questions over whether the band had a future together.

Just twelve months earlier the band had been ecstatically ruling Planet Pop. What had prompted so many doubts over the future of One Direction, and what had made Niall, of all people, so seemingly unhappy with his lot? The short answer was that the band had reached such heights that even the most committed and optimistic in their team had not imagined possible. This was uncharted and unexpected territory. While all concerned were, for the most part, coping well, there seemed to be cracks appearing where the element of fear came to the surface. Niall's tweets from the Miami hotel were, more than any, a signpost that care had to be taken amid the fun.

And what fun they were having! The band visited a casino in Australia. While Niall stopped gambling early in the evening, he has hinted that some of his bandmates were less cautious. He said, 'Like most of the stupid things we do, it seemed like it was a good idea at the time. We just thought, "We're eighteen, this is the first time we've been able to spend a bit of money in weeks because we've been on the road." I won £100, which seemed reasonable, then I stopped. But I'll have to say, "No comment" about the others.' He did not comment but he hinted heavily what happened during the rest of the evening and the aftermath. 'Let's just say it got a bit ugly and a lot of money was lost. A lot. When our management found out, we got a serious dressing-down about it.'

Lest Niall forget for a moment of the scale of his fame, he was reminded in spades when, in April, he went to the dentist to have his braces removed and the story in the *Daily Mail* became the cause of astonishing excitement and importance. As he travelled to the dentist for the procedure, he tweeted his fans with, 'Morning! This is it! I'm goin to the dentist! I think this is my last hour with braces! Oh how I'm gona miss them! Naaaaaaat!' After the dentist, he went for a celebratory meal at Wagamama, which was photographed and written about by newspapers across the world. The newly braceless Niall ordered a selection of starters, followed by chicken katsu curry. The press saw fit to devote space to the fact that he requested that the salad garnish be left off his main course. An earth-shattering development, clearly! Just days later his plastic dental retainer was reduced to a melted ball after staff in a

Berlin hotel placed it in a glass of warm water.

He also had a close shave with a tattooist who rejected his request to ink his bum. Noting, according to the *Daily Mail*, that Harry seemed 'to get a new tattoo every day', Niall had decided to visit a Los Angeles tattoo artist. He wanted to get 'Made In Ireland' tattooed in green on his cheeks, but after he dropped his trousers and pants he was told the plan was a no-goer. 'They said, "The skin on your arse is too squidgy. It needs to be tight."' Perhaps, he later reflected, he had got a lucky escape. 'I suspect they did me a favour,' he continued. 'It wasn't the best idea in the world.' (As well as describing his bum as 'squidgy', Niall has also said he is the owner of 'chicken Irish legs', which risk sunburn if exposed on a sunny day.) For a substantial number of the One Direction fans, this came as good news. Some were feeling that the band, and Harry in particular, were getting too many tattoos.

When subsequent reports claimed that Niall was close to getting a tattoo, he took to Twitter to blast the rumours. 'By the way I didn't get a tattoo! Not plannin either,' he wrote. A little while later, he sent a more angry, yet ultimately ambiguous, message out. 'Some people are sooo disrespectful! Never heard anything like that in my life!' he stormed, in an almost Louis-esque online outburst. Separate rumours had circulated that Niall had been tattooed in tribute to manager Simon Cowell, but this was just the result of a joke on Niall's own part. 'It says I love SC and it's on my bum,' he quipped. For many fans, the longer Niall's body remains uninked the better. Long may that bum remain squidgy.

His squidgy backside has become the source of fascination to the teenage media, with the popular Sugarscape website even devoting an in-depth article to it. 'Niall Horan's bum: 10 things you need to know about it,' ran the attention-grabbing headline. Some of the entries were more serious than others. The only band member to rival Niall in the butt popularity stakes is Louis, about whose bum entire Tumblr accounts are dedicated. Newspapers even reported that Louis had, à la Beyoncé, had his much-admired backside insured. However, Louis himself scotched the rumour in an interview with Washington DC radio station Hot 99.5. 'Very funny story, but why?' he asked. 'I'm not gonna lose it, am I? Why insure it?'

There was more talk about Niall's naked body when a photograph emerged online which purported to show him in the shower. Naturally, it was soon being frantically circulated, viewed and discussed by the band's millions of followers. The physique on show in the snap was certainly one any young man would be proud to have – yet Niall was quick to clarify that it did not belong to him. 'That's not me by the way in that pic!' he tweeted. 'I'd be happy with biceps like that though to be fair!'

Speculation over whom Niall might be dating continued to soar during 2013. Given his private approach to his romantic life, Niall prompted ever-growing fascination with his personal affairs. The less he showed of his private life to the media, the more the media wanted to see it. A celebrity he was regularly linked with was American singer and *X Factor* judge Demi Lovato. It would be a match made in show-business heaven. However, speaking to *Company* magazine, Lovato raged against the rumour. 'I'm so tired of that!' she said. 'It never happened. Niall's a really sweet guy and I definitely consider him a friend, but it's never crossed that line . . . He's a sweet kid and we have an understanding, but we're just friends.'

A source in *Heat* magazine claimed that Simon Cowell had encouraged the pair to become an item, in the knowledge that it would create publicity for two of his key projects: One Direction and *The X Factor*'s USA franchise. 'Demi is being spurred on by Simon, who finds the whole thing very amusing,' an 'insider' claimed in the magazine. 'He's also adoring the publicity it's giving both his band and *The X Factor* – it's a win–win.'

Indeed, Demi backed up this denial a few weeks later during an interview with *Heat*, in which she touched on the sort of pressure that any liaison with Niall carries. Asked whether they still hung out together, she said, 'Not really. Unfortunately, as sweet as he is, it's hard to maintain a friendship with somebody that you really can't hang out with without people automatically assuming that you're dating . . . People tweeted and either said really nice things or rude things. More nice than bad, I guess.'

For Lovato, an internationally famous pop singer and judge on the USA's *X Factor*, to be shocked by the level of pressure around Niall gives the clearest insight yet into how his day-to-day life goes. To be clear, Lovato is very fond of Niall and feels he is a special member of a special band. 'All of the One Direction guys are great, but there is something a little special about him. Niall is one of the most fun people to be around,' she told the *Sun*. 'I know when a text comes through from Niall there is a great chance it is going to actually make me laugh out loud.'

Niall, a longtime fan of Justin Bieber, reportedly got a chance follow in his hero's footsteps romantically. After actress Selena Gomez broke up with Bieber in 2013, she sent feelers out to Niall for a possible date. *NOW* magazine quoted an insider as saying, 'Not only are they friends, but Niall's keen to avoid any trouble with Justin. He knows dating Selena could've prompted a war with Justin.' Soon, Gomez would reportedly have returned to Bieber. Niall, too, would be busy elsewhere, according to the rumour mill, when he reportedly began dating the Irish model Zoe Whelan. He was said to have met Whelan backstage at one of the boy band's gigs. 'Niall has been secretly seeing Zoe for a couple of months after he met her backstage,' a source told the *Sun*. 'She's a Dubliner but is based in London to work on her modelling career. Zoe's travelled all over the UK to meet up with Niall on the band's tour. But the biggest sign he's really serious about her is that he introduced her to his whole family at his brother's wedding.

'Zoe's the first girlfriend Niall has brought back to his hometown of Mullingar since making it big, so it was a big deal and the talk of his family at the wedding. Niall's protective of her as she's shy, but his family all really took a shine to Zoe.'

The curse of being linked romantically to a member of 1D struck Whelan as soon as the stories were published, as she later explained during an interview with the *Herald*. 'The reaction to modelling has been positive by and large,' she told the newspaper. 'I love modelling – who wouldn't like getting paid to look good? A lot of girls have said nice things. But you get nasty and mean comments. I've had a few death threats, which is really scary. I just ignore them; I try not to pay them any attention.' She admits she likes One Direction's music but says the truth of whether she and Niall have been an item is a 'secret'.

He had another option on the cards after Louise Thompson, the star of TV show *Made in Chelsea*, told *New!* magazine, 'I would share a Coke with Niall from One Direction because I have a massive crush on him. But shhh, that's a secret!' the *Sun* claimed that, enthralled by Niall's 'Irish gift of the gab', she traded tweets and then text messages with him. One evening, it is claimed, Niall sent a car to collect her and bring her to his home. According to subsequent reports, she did spend an evening with Niall – but insisted he was a 'friend' and that she 'didn't fancy him'. During the evening, though, she had texted her friend Roise Fortescue, saying she was having the best time of her life, and that Niall was playing guitar for her. Louise's *Made in Chelsea* co-star Andy Jordan confirmed to *New!* that Louise had spent the night with another man, and though he refused to confirm that it was Niall, he did say that he had 'put his foot down' now and that their relationship was stronger. 'Obviously, it was a big blow to our relationship – a disaster,' he admitted. 'But our relationship has got stronger. It was make or break but in a weird way it's made us much tighter.'

On and on the rumours came, but impenetrable mystery surrounded the extent, if any, of Niall's romantic activities during this period. Indeed, according to an unnamed 'friend' of Niall, quoted in the *Sun*, he was 'raging' at a sex ban that had been imposed on the unattached members of the band. '[Niall's] raging about it, all the lads are,' said the friend. 'Four of them are single and they've been told to stay that way as it appeals to their American teen fans. Niall's fighting off the women with his Irish accent and good looks, so he's having to live like a monk.'

The friend continued, 'Niall and the boys are being kept on a really tight leash and it is tough for them. But they are so determined to make it work in the States they'll do whatever they are told. Quite simply a sex scandal over there would be the end of the band.'

Niall had to content himself with the fans in Sweden who had 'flashed' the band to such an extent that, as Harry memorably put it, 'nipple marks' were left on the windows of the band's car. Asked later whether he remembered the 'Swedish flashers', Niall replied, 'Yeh, I do.' However, as Niall told the *Sun*, he did have to tread carefully when it came to women. 'We get a lot of attention from female fans and we have to be careful not to get in trouble,' he said. He was also advised to be cautious when it came to the spending of the increasing fortune he was amassing. 'We've all earned good money too, so we have to be sensible about that when all you can think about it going mad and spending it in a day,' he said.

To clarify his relationship status, at the end of May he tweeted, in reply to a fan's question about a rumoured relationship, 'no Im a single Pringle! And I ironically i like Pringles too.' Yet as he would regularly be reminded, it took very little for tongues to start wagging over his love life. In June he sent a harmless enough tweet to Irish television presenter Glenda Gilson. It read: 'gilson what's the Craic? Haven't heard from ya in ages! How's things?' In very little time at all the fact that he had tweeted her was sparking speculation that they were, or could become, an item. Gilson was on a flight as Niall's tweet to her became a trending topic on Twitter. She had quite a shock when, after landing, she switched her phone back on found herself at the centre of a social networking frenzy.

Niall took a witty swipe at the endless speculation over his love life when he told Sugarscape that he had received many marriage proposals from fans. 'I've got about seven wives at this stage. I might have to get them annulled before I actually get married; it's not good, you know . . .'

Further rumours to circulate around 1D in the first half of 2013 included: that the band probably includes one gay member, according to *N Sync's Lance Bass; that the band would employ the services of the security team that protects US president Barack Obama; that Zayn Malik wanted to become a boxer, thus threatening the beautiful face so beloved of fans around the world; and that the huge fame they had acquired was 'messing with their heads', according to re-formed 1990s boy band 5ive. Elsewhere, it was suggested the band had been put on a hardcore diet for their world tour and that UK Prime Minister David Cameron had 'overruled' his civil servants, who had advised him not to hug Harry in the video for 'One Way or Another (Teenage Kicks)'.

The media obsession with the band spread to unlikely outlets, the *Daily Telegraph*, of all newspapers, suggested Niall and his four fellow band members were turned away from an exclusive members' club in London as they were dressed too casually. The disappointed stars were reportedly barred from entering 5 Hertford Street in Mayfair. Cheesily, according to onlookers, the venue's doorman Claud Achaume said, 'They're going in one direction, and that's away from here.'

Newspapers also reported that One Direction's management had been forced to hire a new security guard to protect the band's clothes – it was suggested that even Niall and co.'s dirty underwear was being pilfered by fans.

In March 2013, there was time for Niall to return to (relative) normality and his family roots, when his brother Greg got married in Ireland. Niall looked stunning in the a three-piece suit he wore to St Michael's Church in Castletown Geoghegan in County Westmeath. With his hair longer than for some time and brushed up, and with some flowers stuck to the lapel of his jacket, he cut quite the dapper and grown-up best man, a role Greg had proudly handed to him. Niall topped off the look with a candy-pink-striped tie. As he pulled up in a Range Rover, he noticed that some One Direction fans had turned up to wait near the church. While he could have been justified in feeling aggrieved that fans had shown up to such a personal occasion, he waved at them as he arrived and then made his way over to give them hugs and sign autographs after the ceremony had finished. Paparazzi were also present, albeit less unexpectedly.

When it was revealed that, with Greg set for fatherhood, Niall was to become an uncle, Directioners around the world came out with a huge 'awwww' of affection. The ever-admiring Sugarscape website declared, 'Niall Horan is going to be the best uncle ever' and listed ten reasons why it believed this to be the case. Most of these reasons were tongue-in-cheek, including: he will explain the facts of life using a plate of Nando's; he will teach any relations valuable life lessons like not to mess with squirrels; that he looks like Uncle Waldo from *The Aristocats*. Yet, amid the humour, there was a tidal wave of support and love for the fact Niall would soon have a niece or nephew. Having dubbed Cowell 'Uncle Simon', Niall was now becoming one himself. It almost felt as if the entire band and their fan base took a step up in age as a result.

Controversy was never far away, though. The crazy intensity of their fame was underlined afresh when some 'fans' published death threats on Twitter aimed at Liam's Siberian Husky dog Loki. 'The dog is not going to see tomorrow if i can help it,' wrote one. 'U were supposed to come back for me liam.' Then some One Direction fans attempted to get the hashtag #dieloki trending. Then, singer-songwriter Jake Bugg launched an angry volley at the band after learning that some commentators were referring to them as 'rock stars', amid reports of wild backstage frolics. 'Who the f**k is saying that?' Bugg asked *ShortList* magazine. 'Oh, I'm pretty sure they have a good laugh. But it's easy to, isn't it? When you don't have to write any songs. 'People [call them the new Beatles] because they broke America, but that don't mean a thing.' He had not finished: 'I mean, [One Direction] must know that they're terrible. They must know . . . Calling them the new rock stars is a ridiculous statement. And people should stop making it.'

Niall was disappointed. He is a fan of Bugg, which meant the singer's words hurt him all the more. 'Really buggs me that artists we're fans of, flip on us in the press!' he wrote on Twitter. Louis followed up with a characteristically less measured Tweet: 'Hi @JakeBugg do you think slagging off boy bands makes you more indie?'

In truth, the comparisons with the Beatles have always had a problematic dimension for the band. Rarely have they explicitly entertained the comparison. 'We watched that film of the Beatles when they first touched down in America and we saw a real likeness with our personalities,' said Harry. Niall agreed, saying: 'They loved having a laugh like us.'

Of more interest than what Bugg and the band themselves think of the comparison is what Beatle Paul McCartney makes of it all. 'The boys are doing great in the States,' he told *Playlist*. 'There's been comparisons made with the Beatles when we first went over there. It takes me back.' He has seen 'so many bands' landed with the title of 'the next Beatles', including Niall's beloved Oasis. However, McCartney feels it is a burden. 'It's a pressure, because suddenly you've got to live up to all the things that we did, and it's a different time. So let's just call them "the next terrific band".'

American media commentator Mike Raia also voiced concern. 'One Direction are being touted here as the Beatles of their generation. That's one heavy load to bear. There is a definite risk of burnout unless they are allowed some time off to let off steam. It would be heart rending to see them fall apart.' *Rolling Stone* magazine had noted that the management were working the band to an 'insane' degree, treating them 'like dogs'.

Not all of Niall's heroes let him down, though. When he met Don Henley and Timothy B. Schmit of the Eagles, a favourite band of his, they happily posed for a photograph with him. 'I met my all time music heroes today "the eagles"!' Niall tweeted. 'Well two of them! Don Henley and Timothy b shmit !#goosebumps.' Weeks later, when rumours circulated that the rock act were planning a summer tour, Niall tweeted his excitement, including a saucy quip: 'Hope the eagles go back on the road . . . cant wait. i'll be there starkers at the front! Hahahaha.'

Furthermore, Justin Young of the indie band the Vaccines gave Niall and bandmate Harry his approval after they worked in the studio together. The perhaps unlikely trio decided to spend some studio time together after they bonded over their love of the indie group the Cribs. The Vaccines' man was impressed by Niall and Harry. 'They are both natural writers. I love writing songs and love pop music, so the process was exciting,' Young told MTV News. 'I don't think they're going for a heavier, indie sound. Maybe it's damaged my credibility, but it wasn't the Vaccines who wrote for them, it was me, so I doubt it's damaged the band's.' He added that he was 'excited' to be working with them.

The band sparked deeper controversy themselves when Niall and Louis both told the *Metro* that, were it not for the band, they would be criminals. Asked what he would be doing if he had not found fame, Louis said, 'I would be struggling my way through education or a life of crime.' Departing from his usual fine PR ways, Niall struck a similar chord. 'I would have been at university, and a life of crime as well,' he said. It was left to Liam to smooth things over. In answer to the same question, he said, 'If One Direction never happened I would be working in a factory or as a fireman.'

Niall's dream job, had he not made it as a pop star, would have been that of a footballer, so he was himself beyond excited when he and his bandmates were invited by football manager José Mourinho to have a kickabout at the Real Madrid training ground. This was every football fan's dream come true. Niall, accompanied by Louis and Liam, could hardly get there quickly enough. They enjoyed a half-hour play with the entire Real squad, and they gave Mourinho some tickets for their concert at the Palacio Vistalegre arena that night. 'Mourinho's daughter is a fan and he wanted to get tickets to the show, so he invited us down to train with the lads,' said Niall in the *Sun*. 'Next thing we were taking free kicks with Ronaldo and Kaká – it was unbelievable. It was all a bit mad. It's really hard to believe the stuff we get to do, it's crazy.'

There was more football-based excitement for Niall when he watched the Republic of Ireland draw with England at Wembley Stadium. The FAI – the Irish football governing body – presented him with a new Irish replica jersey and he stayed in London all week so he could attend the big game in Wembley along with 12,000 other Irish supporters. He expressed his pride and excitement on Twitter. 'Super proud to be Irish! Great game at Wembley! Lads played their socks off! #boysingreen. Thousands of Irish flew in for the game! Great scenes! Shane Long was on fire . . . centre halves didn't know what to do with him . . . crackin' goal too. Had goosebumps listening to the Irish singing The Fields of Athenry! What a great country we are from! Love Ireland so much!'

Niall showed again that he had not lost touch with his Irish roots when he played a short, impromptu pub show in his hometown. He seemed a touch tipsy as he sang, yet that only served to make the experience more touching and authentic. The pub, in the Irish capital of Dublin, was packed. The One Direction fan who posted the video online was clearly overwhelmed by the experience, typing: 'Too much for me! I'm crying! Why Niall James Horan, why? You are my little Irish snowflake and keyboard is full of tears!'

It had been Niall who had been shedding tears as he sang 'Little Things' at a show in Glasgow just weeks earlier. As they performed the hit, he and Zayn were both overcome with emotion. He enjoyed another short break at home at the end of May. While Harry attended his mother's wedding, Niall headed home to Ireland for a relaxing, low-key time. 'I love when I do sweet F all on my days off!' he Tweeted. 'Hit a few golf balls from my garden to a field today and that's as exciting as my day is.' He added, 'Won't be at home for a long time now! Gona miss the family and the lads! Very limited time with them! But #TMHT [*Take Me Home Tour*] is going to Mexico!'

Niall was reminded afresh of the fine dividing line fate can draw when Jordan O'Keefe, whom he had briefly met while queuing for his *X Factor* audition, found some fame of his own via another Cowell-run competition, *Britain's Got Talent*. Remembering how he had spoken to Niall in the queue, O'Keefe told the *Sun*, 'He went on to find fame in One Direction and I went home and cried after not getting through. It was so hard.' For years, O'Keefe was plagued by Horan's ascendancy, starting from the broadcast of *The X Factor*. 'I kept seeing him when boot camp was on TV and told my mum that was the boy I'd met. When he got through to the final I was so happy for him but it was quite hard to watch and see him go on to so much success.

'He was much more confident and a bit more mature than me in that audition but it did make me think, if only

I'd have got through, I could have ended up in the biggest boy band in the world. It drove me on and made me try harder. It made me think if he can do it so can I. If I go on to have half his success then I will be so happy.'

Niall has tried to help out other Irish acts, including, in June 2013, throwing his weight behind the Dublin band Kodaline. As the band released their debut album *In a Perfect World*, Niall tweeted, 'Uk! @Kodaline need your help t get t #1 this week with there album! Go get it!' After the band thanked him via their Twitter account, he replied, '@Kodaline it's an unbelievable album! Class act you lads are! #doinitfortheirish'.

Many an act would covet a Twitter plug from Niall, who has, at the time of writing, some 12 million followers. His plug helped the band reach No. 3 in the album charts.

Irish lads have a fine recent track record in the British pop charts. Boyzone, who were at their peak during the mid-1990s, were an Irish five-piece managed by a pre-*X Factor* Louis Walsh. They sold 25 million records worldwide. Yet even that magnificent figure was dwarfed by Westlife. Also managed by Walsh, this Irish five-piece ultimately sold 40 million records worldwide and had fourteen No. 1 singles in the UK alone. Speaking on RTÉ Two to Westlife star Nicky Byrne, Niall said: 'You struggle to get around town with people taking pictures and that! But that's what I signed up for, I'm not complaining. I've got no problem getting a battered sausage and chips – not too much vinegar, though. More salt!' Not even Take That can rival the Westlife figure, yet if there is one boy band who have a chance of doing so it is One Direction, on whose popularity rests the Irish charm of Niall. Could he yet become Ireland's most prolific pop export?

Relaxing moments for Niall were few and far between. Even when he was at leisure, he could never truly escape the mania surrounding One Direction. Andy Brown, the lead singer of Lawson, gave a vivid insight into Niall's day-to-day existence when he described a night out with the young Irishman. While he was recording in Sweden, Brown was pleased to discover that One Direction were, too. He sensed an opportunity to let his hair down and that was just what he did.

'I ended up going on the lash with Niall,' he said. 'Irish people love a drink and so do Scousers, so we ended up getting bevvied up together. That's why we got on so well.' However, amid the fun and rapport, Brown was surprised by the level of security around Niall. 'He was so down to earth but they had an unbelievable level of security,' he said. 'We were driven underground, snuck through a back entrance and had our own area in the club with free drinks. It was like a military operation.'

As Niall prepared for the band's world tour, he looked on course to give that position a pop. He tweeted: 'Never felt happier . . . just about to embark on a world tour! and its all thanks to you guys! we love you so much!'

As they prepared to tour Mexico, Niall had his mind on food as ever. He whipped up a fajitas-and-rice snack. He proudly shared a photograph of the meal on Instagram and Twitter, with the caption 'cooked by chef Horan'. When they arrived in Mexico, Niall was so jetlagged that his eyes, he tweeted, were 'stinging with tiredness'. Indeed the band were all tired – so much so that Liam took to Twitter to ask fans outside their hotel to keep the noise down. The member known widely as the 'Daddy' of the band wrote, 'Trying to sleep through people shouting names .... Jet lag hurts at this point.'

The tour seemed to generate more and more headlines. The media speculated that Niall had been crying as the band sang the Ed Sheeran heartbreak track 'Moments' – though it may have been that he was simply struggling to get the lines out. Louis had, though, also looked emotional on the night. 'Throat is so sore today! Fingers crossed for tonight! Shittin it.' He added, 'If I sound terrible tonight! Don't judge.' When it was rumoured that he was drunk on stage in Louisville later in June, an angry Niall took to Twitter to deny the claim. 'I'm clearing this one up now!'

he said. 'This bull about us being drunk on stage! No way is that true! Ever, ever! Who is making this s**t up? We give our best on stage every night! And for 1 person to start a rumour! Just messes it all up.'

The source of the rumour had been close-up footage shot by a fan at the concert. After taking a swig from a bottle with clear liquid in it, Niall shook his head theatrically and passed the drink to Louis, who also trembled after taking a gulp. Amateur lip readers suggested that, as he passed the bottle to Louis, Niall had told his bandmate it was vodka.

'Ah now I get why people are saying it! Hahah! Me and @ louis_tomlinson do that every night!' he added afterwards. 'Pretend there is something in the water bottles.'

After calming down, he added, 'Right I'm going back t sleep! Rant over! back to being nialler!'

Lest it appear that he was getting too serious in his life, Niall was soon featured dancing with a pair of underpants on his head. Bandmate Harry uploaded the amusing video featuring Niall dancing backstage with a pair of white pants on his head and a white sock over each hand. He and Harry also 'twerked' on stage in Miami, throwing the fans into ever higher frenzies of excitement.

In July the band dropped a veritable bombshell via YouTube when they announced that their next single would be called 'Best Song Ever'. On the video Niall says,

'Hi, guys, it's us again. We've got a little secret we've been keeping and we want you to be the first to know about it.'

The announcement came as they unveiled the official trailer for their movie, *This Is Us*. The three-minute-twelve-second video thrilled their fans. Niall's was the first band voice heard on it. He was featured telling the fans, 'Because of you, we're number one in thirty-seven countries' – his Irish lilt pronouncing 'thirty' more like 'tirty'. Later in the trailer he revealed he was kicked out of class at school 'for singing Irish traditional songs'. He is also featured claiming that 'we're normal people doing an abnormal job'.

Is he right? Is he normal – and are his band normal? Who are One Direction and where does Niall fit in? Niall conjured a fine answer to that question in the *Daily Mirror* when he compared the band to a twenty-first-century icon, the cast of *The Inbetweeners*. 'They are all a similar age to us,' said Niall. 'Our life is like an extended *Inbetweeners* movie. There are not many eighteen-year-old fellas who can say they've travelled the world so it's pretty crazy.'

He said that, as time has moved on, they have become more familiar with and respectful of one another. 'We've got to the stage now where we know each other's boundaries,' he explained. 'If there's an argument it's over what's on the radio, or, "Turn up the window, it's freezing." Zayn has this thing about getting into the car at six o'clock in the morning and turning the window down. I'm like, "Are you actually serious?!"'

Elsewhere, Niall was the only band member willing to name a bandmate as the grumpiest of One Direction. 'If anyone's likely to bicker in the group, it would be Louis,' he told *Top of the Pops* magazine. And, in an interview with RTÉ Two, he said, 'We do rib each other, saying you have got more followers, it's a bit of a laugh. But I know this sounds like the media-training answer, but I think whatever is good for One Direction is good for me.'

Having survived several predictions of their demise, what comes next for the band? Robbie Williams has compared the band to the biggest UK pop act of recent decades. 'They're quite a power in the way the Spice Girls were,' he told the *Sun*. 'The Spice Girls took over the world and won and I think the One Direction boys have a similar chemistry.' The girl band had six years together in their prime, which would mean that, *if* One Direction were to follow suit, they would, at the time of writing, already be nearly halfway through their life as a band. But, as for the boys themselves, they are always looking ahead, and are hoping for further collaborations with other pop legends of the moment. Perhaps Niall will get the chance to collaborate fully with his long-term hero Justin Bieber. As Niall had queued up for his *X Factor* audition, he'd strummed his guitar and sang 'One Time', Bieber's big hit. He told anyone who would listen that he was proud to be a fan of Bieber and proud to be compared to him.

Now he can count Bieber as a friend, confidant and supporter. Perhaps they will work even more closely in the future. 'We were talking about me collaborating with them on a song on their next album,' said the Canadian of his relationship with the band. 'It's gonna be great.' Bieber also predicts that some other big-name collaborations could be on the cards for the band. 'They sure have an eye for the ladies but, even better for the guys, the ladies have a bit of an eye for them, too,' he continued. From what I hear they shouldn't have much trouble trying to persuade Rihanna, Katy or Taylor to work with them . . . if you know what I'm saying.'

Bieber had Niall's number from the start of One Direction but it is his family, back home in Ireland, who will always know Niall best. To their delight, as they have watched him become one of the planet's most famous young men, he has not strayed from the values they instilled in him. They remain so proud. As his dad Bobby told the *Herald*, 'The good thing is that he's still the same young fella that left our house in Mullingar that day in 2010.'

ONE DIRECTION DISCOGRAPHY

Singles:

'What Makes You Beautiful'	Syco	2011
'Gotta Be You'	Syco	2011
'One Thing'	Syco	2011
'More Than This'	Syco	2012
'Live While We're Young'	Syco	2012
'Little Things'	Syco	2012
'Kiss You'	Syco	2013
'One Way or Another (Teenage Kicks)'	Syco	2013

Albums:

Up All Night	Syco	2011
Take Me Home	Syco	2012

Miscellaneous:

'Heroes' (X Factor Finalists)	2010
'Wishing on a Star'	2011

AWARDS WON WITH ONE DIRECTION

The BRITs

Best Single (for 'What Makes You Beautiful')   2012

Global Success

ARIA Music Awards   2013

Best International Artists   2012

BBC Radio 1 Teen Awards

Best British Album (for *Up All Night*)   2012

Best British Single (for 'One Thing')   2012

Best British Music Act   2012

Billboard Music Awards

Top Duo/Group   2013

Top New Artist   2013

Top Pop Artist   2013

Guinness World Records

First UK group to debut at No. 1 in US   2012

Album Charts

Japan Gold Disc Awards New Artist of the Year	2013
MTV Best Artist of the Year	2012

MTV

Best New Act (Europe)	2012
Best UK & Ireland Act	2012
Biggest Fans	2012

Nickelodeon Kids' Choice

Favourite Music Group	2013
Favourite Song	2013

Nordoff Robbins (music charity)

O2 Silver Clef Award for Ticketmaster	2013
Best Live Act	2013

People's Choice Awards

Favourite Album (for *Up All Night*)	2013
Favourite Song (for 'What Makes You Beautiful')	2013

Radio Disney Music Awards

Best Music Group	2013
Fiercest Fans	2013

Teen Choice Awards
Breakout Group   2012

The *Sun* Bizarre Readers' Awards
Best Pop   2011
Best Pop   2012

BIBLIOGRAPHY

Blair, Linda, *Birth Order* (Piatkus, 2011)

Bower, Tom, *Sweet Revenge: The Intimate Life of Simon Cowell* (Faber & Faber, 2012)

Jepson, Louisa, *Harry Styles – Every Piece of Me* (Simon & Schuster, 2013)

Montgomery, Alice, *Harry Styles: An Unauthorized Biography* (Penguin, 2013)

Newkey-Burden, Chas, *Simon Cowell: The Unauthorized Biography* (Michael O'Mara, 2009)

Oliver, Sarah, *Harry Styles/Niall Horan – The Biography* (John Blake, 2013)

Oliver, Sarah, *One Direction A–Z* (John Blake, 2011)

One Direction, *Dare To Dream: Life As One Direction* (HarperCollins, 2011)

One Direction, *Forever Young: Our Official Story* (HarperCollins, 2011)

Wainwright, Jen, *I Love Niall* (Buster Books, 2013)

White, Danny, *1D: The One Direction Story* (Michael O'Mara, 2012)

PICTURE CREDITS

Page 12: Suzan/EMPICS/PA Images (top); PictureGroup/Rex Features (bottom)

Page 13: © INFphoto.com (top left); Mathew Imaging/ WireImage/Getty Images (top right); Joe Dent/Rex Features (bottom)

Page 14: Madame Tussaud's via Getty Images (top); Everett Collection/Rex Features (centre); Vivid/Rex Features (bottom)

Page 15: Beretta/Sims/Rex Features (top); David Fisher/ Rex Features (bottom)

Page 16: © John Cogill

ACKNOWLEDGEMENTS

Thanks to Katie Duce and Louise Dixon at Michael O'Mara Books.

INDEX

(1D in subentries refers to One Direction)

INDEX

INDEX

INDEX